The Well-Fed Backpacker

The Well-Fed Backpacker

June Fleming

**With Illustrations by
Lauren Jarrett**

VINTAGE BOOKS

A Division of Random House • New York

Third Vintage Books Edition, March 1986

Reprinted by arrangement with Victoria House, Inc., 2218 NE 8th
Avenue, Portland, Oregon.
Portions of this work originally appeared, in slightly different form,
in *Wilderness Camping* magazine.
Cover photograph by Kent and Donna Dannen/Photo Researchers

Library of Congress Cataloging in Publication Data

Fleming, June.
The well-fed backpacker.

Includes index.
1. Outdoor cookery. 2. Backpacking. I. Title.
TX823.F58 1985   641.5'78   84-40660
ISBN 0-394-73804-7

Manufactured in the United States of America
456789

Preface

I have long enjoyed backpacking. There are so many pleasurable aspects: being in grand places that stun you with their beauty, the nestlike coziness of a good bed in your snow camp while a blizzard roars outside, stretching yourself sometimes to the limits of endurance or resourcefulness, the splendid waking process of splashing clear creek water in your face. All these facets of backpacking pleasure came to me in the earliest trail miles I walked and skied.

But the *food*! On these early treks the food was mainly functional, difficult and time-consuming to prepare, generally of mediocre quality and taste, and sometimes downright indigestion-producing. I didn't mind this terribly because I was still having a fine time. But I kept thinking: There must be a better way!

Gradually I gave more thought to what that way might be. I collected ideas from many sources, tried doing as much food-creating as possible and tested methods of organizing that would make for good eating without a lot of work or expense.

After several years of wilderness adventuring, of trial-and-error learning, I reached the point where experience and attitude joined to make eating in the wilds a distinct pleasure, an enjoyable challenge and an integral part of the whole process. I wished there had been a faster, more efficient way to reach that point. I wasn't discouraged from backpacking because of the lengthy learning process, but no doubt many have been.

So, I started sharing some of the learning through a course on backpack foods, and continued learning myself as others shared their ideas. Then came an intensive "practicum" course: a six-week ski trip through Oregon's Cascades with three friends. We needed to plan and package 118 meals to be eaten in a variety of weather conditions. By the time we had gone through the home-preparation phase of those meals, we knew much more than short hikes could ever force us to learn. And an amazing thing happened! We *hadn't* used up the possibilities for good trail foods. We had become creative enough to find new ideas continually popping into our heads!

This book is an outgrowth of all these experiences, an attempt to share some ideas that I hope will increase *your* wilderness pleasure.

June Fleming

Portland, Oregon
April 1976

September 1984, eight years later:

Many moons, many miles, many meals have gone by. With them have come scores of new foods to choose from, dozens of tasty new recipes discovered with good trail friends, a few changes in how we eat and much more learning useful in the backcountry kitchen.

I'm delighted to be able to share with you the bounty of these many wilderness seasons. May it please and fortify you ... body and spirit!

June Fleming

Contents

Introduction

*E*very backpacker, whether beginner or experienced, has his own way of planning and preparing meals for a trip. I want to share with you my way, which is...

- *eclectic* ... drawing ideas from several sources, according to what fits best on a particular trip;
- *not very precise* ... striving for, but not usually worrying about, a good nutritional balance; not fussing much about measurements or cooking techniques;
- *a lot of fun* ... enjoying surprises, sharing, gifting, experimenting. The at-home part of backpacking foods (the creating, the organizing) gives me pleasure;
- *not much work* ... the part of backpack foods that happens on the trail (final fixing and eating) is kept simple and relatively quick;
- *basically creative* ... using some home-dried foods, some wild foods, some homemade foods and a lot of *my* ways of combining or using different foods.

Why should trail food be boring? With a little forethought and effort, the foods you tuck into your backpack will contribute solidly to the total venture, give pleasant surprises, be savored and remembered as part of the many-sided joy of being self-sufficient in the wilds.

Your wilderness pleasure begins long before the trip, as you build your basic fund of knowledge about what foods are available, which are suitable to take in your pack, how to combine them in ways that please you, what equipment fits with your particular style and needs, how to plan ahead so that what remains to be done on the trail is merely simple preparation and full enjoyment.

Your wilderness kitchen, with both its tangible and its intangible equipment, will be ready to go at any time, needing only the addition of a few meals or parts thereof drawn from your store of ideas. You may find yourself gathering food lists, recipes and one-liners (simple combinations of ingredients) into a file folder or notebook labeled Trail Foods, all set to yield inspiration later when you are planning an adventure on Vibram soles or cross-country skis.

Your freezer and cupboards may hold trail-portion packets of a special homemade granola, bars of pemmican, bags of gorp, smoked fish. You may begin to dabble in home-dried foods, thus adding one more dimension to trail eating with shelves stocked with lightweight, tasty and versatile fruits, vegetables, herbs and more.

This kind of approach extends the satisfactions of the wilds to include your at-home days. Now they are tinged with food discoveries to be utilized later. When the muse is with you and as time and budget allow, you can turn an ordinary workday evening or a rainy Sunday afternoon into a chance to prepare for wilderness trips not yet crystallized on your calendar. These practices give something of the same delightful feeling as studying topographic maps in front of your fireplace and learning in January the names and habitats of a dozen new plants you will first see in spring.

You *have* to eat when hiking, backpacking or skiing. But this need not mean chores you'd just as soon avoid, undue expense to gain freeze-dried variety and ease of preparation, or fare that fuels you adequately but bores you in the process. Add something of yourself to the suggestions in these pages, keep on searching for new ideas and the pleasures of eating in the wilds will grow!

The Well-Fed Backpacker

The Well-Fed Backpacker

... *is pleased and satisfied by the part of his wilderness
experiences that have to do with food*

...*has knowledge that enables him to plan, package
and prepare foods for all kinds of trips*

...*has a creative and flexible attitude about what
and how to eat*

... *sees the necessity of eating while adventuring
not as a nuisance, but as another part of the fun*

1

Some Basics

*T*he secret to eating well in the wilds is thinking ahead, developing a few skills and staying flexible. The process builds on what you already have: at least minimal ability to fix food, some creativity, adventurousness and skill at organizing.

Unless you get a kick out of it (or in the few situations where these considerations are vital), you don't really need to dwell heavily on things like exact nutritional balance, paring cost to the bone or being ounce-careful about food weights. If you are in reasonably good physical condition, the effects of a somewhat unbalanced diet will hardly begin to show on trips of a week or less in mild weather.

But add factors such as prolonged or strenuous exertion or severe weather conditions and your nutritional intake becomes crucial. In addition to having reduced stamina, a poorly fueled hiker is much more susceptible to hypothermia, frostbite and injury. And not only is he more likely to get into trouble, he simply won't enjoy the days if his food intake is poor.

On *long* trips food weight is obviously a prime consideration. You will probably be carrying extra pounds of equipment as well as more food, so it's good to be versatile enough that you can eat foods that are both good *and* light.

Sometimes the cost factor might keep you home if your options are limited to expensive freeze-dried foods and there's no money to spare when you want to hike.

If you find that you need or want detailed information on nutrition, cost and weights, there are some excellent aids, such as the food section in Robert S. Wood's *Pleasure Packing for the 80's*, or in publications of the U.S. Department of Agriculture.

High-protein meatless cooking is a natural for backpackers, since meat is perishable and not as easy to include in trail foods as it is at home. And recent years have brought two developments nudging many toward decreasing their overall meat intake: soaring prices and a greater awareness of what is good for our bodies. The benefits of learning how to get enough protein from sources other than meat spill over from home to the wilds. Two books that provide abundant ideas you can adapt are *Recipes for a Small Planet* by Ellen Buchman Ewald and *Laurel's Kitchen* by Laurel Robertson, Carol Flinders and Bronwen Godfrey.

FIRING YOUR ENERGY MACHINE: NUTRITIONAL NEEDS

Moderate backpacking boosts caloric needs at least 1,000 calories a day above normal requirements, and the more vigorous the activity level, the more calories your energy machine burns. That can mean an extra 2,000 to 3,000 calories a day when hiking hours of demanding terrain with a heavy pack. More body fuel is also needed in cold weather than in mild.

What your body doesn't get from food intake, it will get by burning fat. Most of us aren't hurt by a little hunger and weight loss, but wilderness trips aren't the time to diet. Feeling weak and dragged out doesn't match with the upbeat, vivid experience of wilderness travel.

Some people react to high elevations and exertion with dulled appetites. If you're one of them, make yourself eat adequately anyway to keep up your stamina and resilience. If you don't, you'll have less fun and could be in real jeopardy should illness, injury or other adversity hit.

Your caloric intake should be about half carbohydrates and one-quarter each fats and proteins. Carbohydrates provide quick energy and an immediate lift to lagging bodies. They are also easily digested, a plus during vigorous activity. But the energy from carbohydrates doesn't last long, so you also need the slower but more long-term benefits of proteins and fats.

These both require more time and effort to digest, so they shouldn't be eaten in large quantities, especially during or before strenuous exertion. Chocolate, the mythical high-energy boost, can cause digestive discomfort if large amounts are used as snacks during strenuous exercise; it has a high fat content.

Spread your intake of proteins and fats throughout the day, rather than concentrating them in one heavy meal. Frequent nibbling on a trail mix that contains nuts, dried fruits and chocolate or carob bits makes great sense.

Sometimes, such as in very cold weather or in a survival situation, you may need both quick energy and long-lasting energy.

Then candy will give your body an immediate boost in terms of temperature and energy, but cheese or jerky will do more to fuel you through a long period of inactivity.

Some major sources of *carbohydrates* are: cereals, grains, fruits, vegetables, pasta, honey, candy, fruit drinks. Good sources of *fat* are: butter, margarine, oil, cheese, peanut butter, nuts, coconut, chocolate, sesame and sunflower seeds. *Proteins* are found in: meat, fish, cheese, milk products, eggs, nuts, seeds, peanut butter, the complementary combinations of grains, legumes and milk products.

With this basic knowledge of nutritional needs, and with the variety and pleasure that most of us like in foods, it is likely that the trail menus we devise will supply most needed nutrients.

WHAT MAKES A GOOD HIKING FOOD?

Fundamentally, whatever serves your purpose for a given trip is the right food to take. There are some qualities that *usually* describe good hiking food:

- nutritious
- easy to fix
- quick
- lightweight
- tasty
- compact and sturdy
- not too costly
- nonperishable

Those make sense. BUT . . . there are no hard-and-fast rules about creative trail cooking! On some of your trips you can completely ignore certain "ideal" food qualities because the structure and purpose of the adventure allows it.

There are times when one or two of the basic qualities listed above are the deciding factors in your menu planning. A week-long ski trip, for instance, won't allow for the fresh steaks and heavy bottle of wine with which you celebrate a special friendship on a summer weekend hike. But in cold-weather camping you are traveling in a huge refrigerator and can enjoy the luxury of many foods that would be too perishable on summer treks (such as fresh meat, eggs, fruits and vegetables).

Sometimes you will want the food to be one of the highlights of a trip, as when you are base-camping and setting a more leisurely pace, with time for fishing, plant study or lolling in the sun. At other times you may look at food mainly as adequate fuel for prolonged, strenuous activity, and so forgo a luxury food that takes more pack space or preparation time. (On the other hand, your spirits may need that luxury now and then!)

If variety is so important to you that you would feel bored and oppressed by repeating the same main dish every night for a week, then you'll probably do something about it. What you'll do is invest a considerable amount of ingenuity and some advance effort so that variety will be the result. In the process you'll be rewarded by an increasing level of resourcefulness and a lot of pure fun.

Eating in the wilds and *eating at home* differ in several ways:

- A three-meals-a-day structure won't feel comfortable or meet the fueling needs of a backpacker.
- Because many hiking foods are concentrated and have much of their moisture removed, you won't feel as full as after high-bulk city meals.
- After an initial adjustment period, you may eat more or less on the trail than you do at home. On a six-week trip I ate about half again as much as my at-home intake and still lost a few pounds. I've hiked with others whose appetite is diminished by exertion, especially during a trip's first day or two.
- When active, you will need more carbohydrates (not more protein) than usual; in cold weather, more fats to stoke your body furnace.

DIFFERENT WAYS TO GO

There is a wealth of possible "styles" available to the backpacker. Depending on how much he wants to spend in time and money, prepare in advance or do for himself, he can choose from:

- freeze-dried foods (individual items or whole meals)
- home-prepared things (granola, fruit leathers, Russian Tea, brownies)
- grocery store foods (macaroni and cheese, instant pudding, oatmeal)

He can do most or all the preparation himself or pay for someone else to do it. He can use expensive freeze-dried foods almost exclusively, avoid them altogether or use some selectively. He can choose all no-cook foods for a trip in mild weather, avoiding the time-fuss-weight of cooking and its gear. He can plan some quick meals and some that require more preparation. In short, there is no *one* way that is always best!

COSTS AND WEIGHTS

These will vary with the style you choose, but you can reasonably expect to eat well carrying 1½ to 2 pounds of food per person per day and spending $5.00 per person per day; this includes all meals and snacks. By planning very carefully and doing much preparation in advance yourself, you can keep costs and weights down even more. If you go to the prepackaged-meals route at the outdoor store, costs can easily double. For instance, a prepackaged breakfast for four of pancake mix, syrup mix, juice, beef sticks, cocoa and cooking oil costs around $9.50.

PREPACKAGED BREAKFAST
cost for four: $9.50

By packaging the same meal yourself, you can save over half the cost!

ASSEMBLE YOUR OWN BREAKFAST

pancakes (an add-only-water mix)	.55
syrup (brown sugar, margarine,	
maple flavoring)	.42
juice (powdered)	.80
beef sticks	1.19
vegetable oil	.05
cocoa	.60
Total	$3.61

A prepackaged dinner for four consisting of chicken noodle soup, rice and chicken, peaches and fruit drink costs $11.50.

PREPACKAGED DINNER

cost for four: $11.50

By simply gathering the separate items at the grocery store and doing a minimum of repackaging, costs drop by more than a third. The savings could be even greater if you dried your own fruit and put together a dried garden soup blend.

ASSEMBLE YOUR OWN DINNER

soup	1.00 (or less)
rice and chicken	4.28
(breakdown below)	
dried peaches	1.20 (or less)
fruit drink	.40

rice and chicken you put
together yourself:

quick rice	1.20
canned chicken	2.29
sour cream sauce mix	.69
instant dry milk for mix	.10
Total	4.28

There are other benefits besides saving money when you put together your own backpack foods. A soup mix made of vegetables and herbs you've grown or dried yourself tastes twice as good as the best any store can sell and is often superior nutritionally as well.

As to weight, a common tendency is to take *much* more food than you need or will eat. (Some sort of primal insecurity seems to take over when we travel out of store range . . . I've probably packed home a cumulative total of 29 pounds of fig bars!) Since backpacking food is often dried or concentrated, that handful of noodles or small package of dried fruit looks deceptively skimpy. In goes another handful for good measure and a bit more fruit, and before you know it, your food supply weighs double what it should.

Sometime, when there is no big risk involved, try paring down your food to just enough for a trip. (Don't count the emergency food you should *always* have in your pack.)

2

~~~~~

Sources of Hiking Foods

*I*t's very easy to plan food for weekend jaunts or trips of several days' duration by relying solely on *one* food supplier. Many hikers never venture beyond the grocery store or the outdoor store for their provisions. This approach looks simplest and therefore has some surface appeal.

- Outdoor store: no time needed for prodding your own imagination; you simply choose from a vast array of packaged meals and snacks contrived by someone else. All you have to do is pick and pay.
- Grocery store: avoid the excessive expense of freeze-dried foods altogether; do your own detailed menu planning and packaging.

In a comparison experiment once, I went to these two main sources most hikers use—grocery store, outdoor store—and at each place I bought enough food for two people for one day of average backpacking. The foods I chose were comparably moderate, with a few luxuries in each group. I could have spent much more or somewhat less at both places. Both assemblages were reasonably lightweight, nutritious, fairly nonperishable, varied, easy and quick to fix.

The main differences were in *cost, time to shop* and *amount of packaging required*. Outdoor-store foods cost about $9 per person; grocery store foods about $5. Shopping was quick and painless at the outdoor store; foods were located in one area and theoretically all suitable for trail use. I spent longer choosing rations from the grocery store, since I needed to sort these foods out from many other unsuitable products.

My packaging efforts were nil with outdoor-store edibles . . . I had paid someone else for his investment of time and energy. I did considerable repackaging of grocery store items, although several were ready to toss into a pack as is. While repackaging, I used the opportunity to customize my provisions with added touches from the kitchen shelves—spices, wheat germ and such.

There are gains and losses inherent in any route you choose if you rely on only *one* source. So why not be flexible and enjoy the advantages each source has to offer while avoiding what may be a disadvantage for one particular time and trip? By putting together ingredients from several sources, you'll frequently come up with delicious dishes that yield more nutritional punch for the penny than ready-made counterparts, cost far less and are often more exciting.

Likely spots to find the goods for your outdoor pantry are the grocery store, natural foods store, deli, ethnic market, outdoor store and, if you're one of the fortunates, your own garden. Look at the offerings of each of these places with an eye to what yields good nutrition quickly and easily and can be combined with other foods in a tempting way.

When you backpack frequently and think often about food for the wilds, you'll begin to build a backlog of ideas and basic foods kept on hand. Planning will spread itself throughout the year, so that when time is ample, you do the more time-consuming preparations. When your creativity runs high, you jot down new recipes and procedures; when money isn't tight, you take advantage of sales to lay in a supply of dried or freeze-dried items. And *always* the wilderness part of your mind leads you to scout

out new possibilities: How could I adapt this dish to the trail? What new items on the grocery store shelves would fit into camp meals? Is it workable to dry this food?

If you decide to put together some of your own main dishes, desserts or whole meals, you can get a lot of ideas by looking at what the outdoor store or catalog has to offer, studying the ingredients, then assembling a reasonable facsimile (maybe even an improvement) of your own. Buy one of each kind of snack bar (such as carob fudge, pemmican, nut bars, sesame wafers) found in the natural foods store, study the ingredients and duplicate it yourself, at a fraction of the cost.

DRY IS LIGHT

It makes sense to use some dried foods, especially if you'll be toting several days' worth of edibles. Dried things are lighter, less bulky, nonperishable. They'll help you eat well while staying within the 2 pounds of food per person per day that's good to shoot for. What's the difference between "freeze-dried" and "dehydrated"?

Freeze-dried foods can only be processed commercially and are .vacuum-packed. They're extremely light and close to their original size. Most reconstitute by sitting in hot water for about 10 minutes; a few (such as ice cream) are meant to be eaten dry. You can get freeze-dried foods at outdoor stores in the form of whole dishes, such as beef Stroganoff, or as separate items, such as meat chunks, veggies or fruits. The rub is their large price tag, upward of $2 a serving for most main dishes, $1 for veggies. Outdoor stores offer both freeze-dried and dehydrated foods . . . read labels to determine which process was used.

Dehydrated foods are less expensive. Their moisture is extracted very slowly, so they shrivel up to a smaller, wrinkled approximation of their original state. Unless the pieces are fairly small or the food very porous, they take a bit longer to rehydrate. But many fruits and even some veggies are edible in dried form, and many rehydrate in just a few minutes. You can buy dehydrated foods in small packages and in bulk, or save money by drying them yourself in a food dryer or your oven. They're easy to fix, delicious and add real spark to your outdoor menus.

RETORT FOODS

There's an array of retort main dishes—precooked, pouch-sealed "5-minute entrees"—sold in both outdoor and grocery stores. Vacuum-sealed, without preservatives, they keep for two years without refrigeration. Each single-serving portion heats right in its foil pouch, submerged in water.

For short trips when you want home-style Swiss steak or chicken cacciatore and don't care about price and weight, retort entrees may tempt you. Each serving costs between $2.25 and $3.25 and weighs 9 ounces. (Comparable freeze-dried servings bear similar price tags, but weigh between 1¾ and 4 ounces.)

Having urged you to be eclectic, here are some ideas about what different sources have to offer. You'll be adding to the lists yourself.

GROCERY STORE

In addition to the usual items, many large grocery stores and produce markets have expanded services and now stock a variety of edibles in bulk. Prices are much lower than for the same foods sold in prepackaged weights: grains, nuts, textured vegetable protein, dried fruit, pancake mix, cooked cereal blends and more.

Breakfast

Hearty cold cereals:
 Granola
 All-Bran
 Bran Buds
 Grape-Nuts
 Familia
Instant or one-minute cereals:
 Instant oatmeal (several flavors, individual packets)
 Quick oatmeal
 Cream of Wheat

Cream of Rice
Malt-O-Meal
Quick-cooking cereals:
 Ralston
 Roman Meal
 Zoom
 Wheat Hearts
 Quick Grits
Quick rice
Toasted wheat germ
Sesame seeds
Sunflower seed kernels
Breakfast bars

Granola bars
Compact breads
English muffins
Muffin mix (several flavors)
Granola bar mix (bake
    ahead)
Pancake mix (buttermilk
    and whole wheat;
    choose an add-only-
    water kind)
Raisins
Dried fruit
Fruit leather
Coconut
Nuts
Melon (heavy, but travels
    well)
Honey
Jam
Brown sugar
Margarine (solid or liquid)
Meat sticks
Canned sliced bacon
Canadian bacon
Smoked sausage links
Jerky
Soy bacon bits
Eggs

Cheese
Dried hash-brown potatoes
Instant dry milk (low-fat
    more nutritious than
    nonfat)
Nondairy creamer
Powdered buttermilk
Instant cocoa (some need
    milk, some just water)
Instant strawberry drink
    (needs milk)
Instant breakfast drink (sev-
    eral flavors, add milk)
Instant malted milk
Ovaltine
Instant coffee
Powdered eggnog drink (in-
    dividual packets)
Powdered spiced cider (in-
    dividual packets)
Tea (bags and instant pow-
    dered)
Powdered breakfast drinks
    (orange, grape, grape-
    fruit)
Fruit juice pouches (several
    flavors, packed with
    straws)

Lunch and Snacks

Cheese (several kinds in
    bulk, bars, slices, cold
    pack, squeeze-packs)
Cream cheese (plain and
    several fancy flavors)
Sturdy crackers (dozens of
    flavors and shapes)
Rice cakes
Rolls

Pocket bread
Bagels (several kinds)
English muffins
Compact breads (rye, pum-
    pernickel, etc.)
Canned brown bread
Peanut butter
Jam
Honey

Jerky (several kinds)
Sliced smoked meats
Dry salami
Pepperoni
Thuringer sausage
Meat sticks
Canned meat spreads
Canned fish (sardines in several sauces, tuna, oysters, kippers)
Vienna sausage
Canned dips (cheese, bean, enchilada)
Boxed jerky seasoning, salami seasoning (use with hamburger, bake ahead)
Powdered soup mixes (dozens of flavors, both standard and exotic; choose instant or ones with 15 minutes' or less cooking required)
Bouillon cubes or powder (beef, chicken, fish, vegetable flavors)
Fresh produce: apples, oranges, carrots, celery, summer squashes
Raisins
Dried fruit

Fruit leather
Condensed mincemeat
Nuts
Sunflower seed kernels
Pumpkin seeds
Coconut chips
Corn nuts
Trail mixes
Sturdy cookies
Candy (bars, packaged and bulk hard candies, jelly beans, licorice, halvah, Life Savers)
Chocolate bits
Butterscotch bits
Granola bars
Instant pudding mix (several flavors)
Canned individual pudding (several flavors)
Instant dry milk
Instant malted milk
Fruit drink powders (with sugar or Nutrasweet)
Fruit drink pouches (several flavors, packed with straws)
Fruit juice pouches (several flavors, packed with straws)

Dinner

Powdered soup mixes (dozens of flavors, standard and exotic; choose instant or ones with 15 minutes' or less cooking time required)

Dips (clam, onion, nacho cheese, guacamole)
Dip mix (several flavors, use with sour-cream sauce mix and instant dry milk)

Cheese (several kinds and forms)
Cream cheese (plain and several fancy flavors)
Rolls
Pocket bread
French bread
Canned brown bread
Corn and flour tortillas
Basic baking mix
Muffin mix (several flavors)
Cornbread/muffin mix
Quick rice (white, brown, wild, several flavors, boil-in-bag; choose those that cook in 15 minutes or less)
Pastas (choose the quickest-cooking forms):
Noodles (several flavors and shapes)
Macaroni (several flavors and shapes)
Spaghetti (egg and whole wheat, several forms)
Ramen noodles (egg, whole wheat, brown rice, buckwheat)
Chow mein noodles
Bulgur wheat
Bean threads
Boxed dinner mixes:
Hamburger Helper (several varieties)
Tuna Helper (several varieties)
Chicken Helper (several varieties)
Rice mixes (several varieties)
Macaroni and cheese (some complete, some need margarine and milk)
Noodle dinners (Stroganoff, lasagna, chicken, almond flavors)
Retort main dishes (single-serving, precooked, boil-in-bag, several entrees)
Fresh produce (heavy, but travels well):
Apples, oranges, lemon (for fish), kiwi fruit, carrots, celery, cucumber, radishes, onions, potatoes, summer squash, avocado, turnips, cabbage, cauliflower, broccoli
Frozen vegetables (for early use on cool-weather trips)
Dried vegetables:
Mushrooms
Onions, chives
Green and red peppers
Soup blends
Potatoes (mashed-potato flakes, shredded, sliced, cubed in boxed mixes with sauce; note: most dried potato mixes aren't practical for trail use because they require long baking times, but you can use the dried potatoes in stove-top dishes such as those in "Dinner Fare," chapter 9.)

Canned meats:
  Boned chicken and turkey, corned beef, luncheon meat, Vienna sausage, ham, sliced dried beef
Canned fish:
  Tuna, salmon, clams, shrimp, crab
Textured vegetable protein ("TVP," a low-cost meat substitute made from soybeans; granular and chunk form; beef, ham, chicken and bacon flavors)
Dried herbs
Spices
Dried orange and lemon peel
Bouillon cubes or powder (beef, chicken, fish, vegetable flavors)
Soy sauce
Margarine (solid and liquid)
Cooking oil
Butter Buds (butter-flavored powder)
Nondairy creamer
Instant dry milk
Sauce and seasoning packets:
  Spaghetti
  Taco
  Sloppy joe
  Chili
  Sour-cream sauce
  White
  Cheese
  Mushroom
  Curry

Stir fry
Beef stew
Meat loaf
Stroganoff
Au gratin
Sweet and sour
Teriyaki (useful as a dry soy sauce substitute)
Miso
Au jus
Gravy (several kinds)
Salad dressing mix
Cracker meal (for fish)
Croutons
Instant coffee (regular and flavored)
Tea (bags and powdered, plain and with lemon)
Fruit drink powders (with sugar or Nutrasweet)
Powdered eggnog drink (individual packets)
Powdered spiced cider (individual packets)
Sturdy cookies
Fruitcake
Crumb crusts
Gingerbread mix
Brownie mix
Snacking cake mix (several kinds)
Frosting mix (several flavors)
Canned pudding (individual, several flavors)
Instant pudding (several flavors)
Pudding requiring cooking (several flavors, including rice)
No-bake custard (requires chilling)

No-bake cheesecake
Fruit gelatin (several flavors,
     with sugar or Nutra-
     sweet)
Danish Dessert (raspberry
     and strawberry)
Whipped topping mix

Magic Shell chocolate syrup
Four-Minute Fudge
Candy bars
Nuts
Popcorn (bulk and Jiffy-pop
     in foil pans)

Note: Don't overlook the gourmet section, which has many suitable items.

OUTDOOR STORE

Freeze-dried, dehydrated and other packaged foods include separate ingredients and complete entrees serving either 2 or 4. (For group trips, freeze-dried foods also come in #10 tins containing 8 large servings.) You can also purchase whole meals—breakfast, lunch and dinner packs that serve 4, as well as single-serving lunch packs—containing everything from beverage to cooking oil. Unopened foil pouches will keep for months without refrigeration.

Whole-meal packs aren't featured as prominently as a few years ago, although the overall variety and number of food items available has increased tremendously. One possible reason: Shoppers are more cost-conscious these days and find that it's often cheaper to buy individual items and assemble their own freeze-dried meals. The sheer variety available also makes choosing more fun!

Another trend noticeable in the outdoor store's food section is the inclusion of *many* natural foods (no preservatives or artificial flavors), such as vegetarian entrees, soups, pilafs and vegetable pasta dishes. You'll also find dozens of gourmet goodies, including fancy coffees (some in individual-serving bags), smoked salmon, gourmet seasoned popcorn, cheese fondu with sherry, cherry–chocolate mousse and the like.

The outdoor store is the only place I've been able to find some very useful dried versions of certain foods: tamari, eggs, cheese spread, peanut butter spread, vegetable juice, tomato (to be reconstituted for juice, sauce or paste).

Keep in mind as you shop that many foods sold in outdoor stores can also be found in grocery stores, with much smaller price tags. Unless you're time-pressed, this is not the place to buy instant dry milk, Butter Buds, fruit drink powders, instant soups in the standard flavors, granola bars, instant cocoa, nuts, candy bars and similar common items.

Hiking Foods from the Outdoor Store

Powdered eggs
Eggs with butter
Eggs with bacon
Cheese omelet
Hash-brown potatoes
Granola with freeze-dried blueberries and milk
Mountain mush
Granola bars
Pancake mix (apple-raisin, blueberry)
Maple syrup granules
Pilot bread
Crackers (several kinds)
Gourmet cheese (several kinds)
Powdered cheese spread
Powdered peanut butter spread
Powdered margarine spread
Jam (individual packets)
Honey (individual packets)
Instant dry milk
Nondairy creamer (individual packets)
Cooking oil
Six-spice dispenser
Powdered tamari
Freeze-dried cottage cheese
Freeze-dried tuna salad
Freeze-dried chicken salad
Dehydrated fruit (single fruits and mixes)

Freeze-dried fruit (single fruits and mixes)
Fruit leather
Trail mix
Nuts
Pemmican bar
Powdered soup (standard and gourmet flavors)
Wine salami
Salmon jerky
Beef jerky
Beef sticks
Meat bar (precooked, compressed)
Bacon bar (precooked, compressed)
Canned bacon
Freeze-dried meats (diced beef, ham and chicken; sausage patties; beef patties)
Retort main dishes (several boil-in-bag entrees, single-serving)
Freeze-dried vegetables (single vegetables, mixes, potatoes with cheese and chives)
Freeze-dried main dishes (many standards, which include meat as well as vegetarian entrees and gourmet treats)

Pasta with sauce (several kinds)

Coffee (standard and fancy in various packs)

Tea (standard, herbal, spiced)

Instant cocoa (individual packets; regular, mint and orange flavored)

Fruit drink powders (individual and 1-quart packets)

Fruit drink pouches (individual servings, packed with straws)

Powdered tomato-vegetable juice (individual packets)

Gourmet seasoned popcorn

Whole wheat fig or apricot bars

Cookies and wafers (many fancy kinds)

Candy (many kinds of bars, including specialties such as mint cake)

Freeze-dried ice cream (eat dry: vanilla, chocolate, strawberry, Neapolitan)

Dessert mixes:
  Mocha mousse
  Cobbler (blueberry, raspberry)
  Pineapple cheesecake
  Apple–almond crisp
  Dessert fritters (walnut, pecan)
  Fruit compote (French apple and others)
  Instant pudding (many flavors)

NATURAL FOODS STORE

The growing number of people who eat unprocessed, healthful foods at home face a dilemma when they hike. Many natural foods—brown rice, beans and such—require long cooking times (and sometimes presoaking), which aren't usually practical in the wilds.

Along with many others, I've changed my eating habits over the past few years and now include many more natural foods in both my city and my wilderness fare. (I'll admit I'm no purist, however. Some refined and processed foods still please me.)

In my search through the palate-boggling array of options available at natural foods stores, I've found there are many foods that *do* work well. That is, they are quick and easy to prepare, as well as being economical. Some, such as dehydrated honey, seem almost designed for backpackers!

Although many items are a bit pricey, bulk stocks of others—spices, grains, seeds, cereal blends, granola, honey, pancake mix and such—offer real bargains.

Hiking Foods from the Natural Foods Store

Oatmeal (including quick)
Cooked cereal mixes (corn bran, oat bran, wheat, etc.)
Cold cereals
Granola (several kinds)
Pancake mix
Powdered egg mix
Syrup (small jars; maple, ginger)
Fresh fruit
Dried fruit
Raisins
Coconut (shredded, flaked; unsweetened)
Fresh vegetables

Dehydrated vegetables (onions, mushrooms, tomatoes, beans, peas, lentils, blends)
Sprout mix
Cheese (dozens)
Powdered soup (several unusual flavors; instant and cooking required— check times)
Dried fish
Sausage
Rolls
Bagels (several kinds)
Compact bread (many, some in small loaves)

Flatbread
Rice cakes
Wafers (sesame, rice, malt)
Crackers (dozens of flavors
    and shapes)
Seeds and meal (sesame,
    pumpkin, sunflower,
    flax, chia)
Nuts (many kinds)
Rice (quick brown)
Grains (check cooking times;
    bulgur, couscous, millet,
    quick-cooking barley)
Pasta (check cooking times;
    macaroni, spaghetti,
    noodles in several
    types—alphabet, ramen:
    whole wheat ramen in
    bulk, several kinds
    packaged with broth/
    seasoning mix, e.g., five-
    spice, curry, miso)
Bean threads
Freeze-dried tofu
Nut burger mix
Pasta Roma (with tomato
    sauce and cheese)
Cheese and herb pasta
Whole wheat macaroni and
    cheese
Couscous pilaf
Backpack vegetarian main
    dishes (no preservatives
    or artificial flavors;
    check cooking time,
    since some are rather
    long)
Tabbouli salad mix (soaks)
Powdered hummus (spiced
    garbanzo bean dip)

Spices
Dried herbs
Miso powder
Carob powder
Soy sauce
Dried seaweed
Gourmet sauces (honey—
    mustard, curry, béar-
    naise, Cheddar, etc.)
Tea (regular and herbal,
    bags and bulk)
Coffee (standard and gour-
    met)
Coffee substitutes (grain
    beverages)
Carob drink mix
Baked dessert cakes (indi-
    vidual portions; carob,
    spice and others)
Carob brownie mix
Carob fudge mix
Cornbread mix
Muffin mix
Fig bars
Granola bars
Date bars
Cookies (many kinds)
Pudding (several flavors,
    quick-cook; check other
    ingredients needed)
Gelatin desserts (several fla-
    vors; some need honey
    added)
Molasses
Peanut butter (also cashew,
    almond)
Honey (regular and dehy-
    drated)
Jam
Turbinado sugar (unrefined)

Date sugar (powdered dehy-
    drated dates)
Carob chips
Cooking oil (soy, peanut, ses-
    ame, safflower)
Instant dry milk
Instant buttermilk

Popcorn
Corn nuts
Energy bars
Mealpack bars
Candy (halvah, sesame wa-
    fers, etc.)

ETHNIC MARKET, IMPORT
STORE, DELI

Many items listed here can also be found in the gourmet sections
of some grocery stores (whose stock varies greatly, depending
on size and location).

Familia
Pancake mix
Potato pancake mix
Muffin mix (several kinds)
Tea (dozens)
Coffee (many)
Fruit drink bouillon (rose
    hip, fruitade, chamo-
    mile)
Instant cocoa
Instant herb beverage
Instant cereal beverage
Rice cakes
Wheat cakes
Sturdy crackers (many
    kinds)
Flatbread
Compact bread (many)
Cheese (many, including
    Brie and Camembert)
Dried fish (many kinds)
Freeze-dried shrimp
Jerky
Canned meat
    (many kinds)

Canned fish (smoked
    shrimp, smoked trout,
    oysters, clams, sardines
    in various sauces)
Powdered soup (dozens of
    standard and gourmet
    flavors)
Bouillon cubes and powder
    (beef, oxtail, chicken,
    fish, vegetable flavors)
Rice
Couscous
Kasha (roasted buckwheat
    kernels, 15 minutes)
Pasta (dozens, many quick-
    cooking; check times)
Gnocchi mix (Italian potato
    dumplings)
Instant noodle dishes
Tabbouli salad mix (soaks)
Couscous pilaf (5 minutes)
Wheat pilaf (15 minutes)
Pasta pilaf (15 minutes; Ital-
    ian, chicken, spicy
    Spanish)

Dehydrated vegetables
  (mushrooms, potatoes
  and others)
Dehydrated seaweed
Spices
Seasoning and sauce packets
  Stir fry
  Sweet and sour
  Chinese barbecue
  Indonesian peanut sauce
  Fried rice
  Chow mein
  Teriyaki
  Curry
  Hollandaise
  Cheese
  White

Vanilla sugar (powdered
  flavoring agent in
  small packets)
Dessert glaze mix
Dessert sauce mix
  (vanilla)
Pudding (several flavors,
  cook)
Candy (large variety)
Cookies (large
  variety)
Energy bars
Popcorn
Nuts
Sesame seeds

3

~~~~~

Menu Planning

*G*ood planning is the first step toward good eating, and the *flexible* planner enjoys it most and gets the best results. Start by chucking any rigid food ideas you might harbor, such as that breakfast is always bacon and eggs or that dinner must have four separate hot parts.

If you try to duplicate city-style meals with several courses exactly, you'll be in for some needless frustration because the conditions and tools you work with are different. I remember a lovely mountain evening marred by the frustration of trying to fix a prepackaged meal of applesauce, green beans, mashed potatoes, and freeze-dried pork chops on *one* stove. Three out of four courses *had* to be cold by the time we ate them, and that far outbalanced the relatively acceptable flavors!

A useful motto: If it's good enough to pack, it's good enough to eat any time of the day. Sturdy cookies and turkey jerky made a great breakfast in bed!

Lest you be tempted or lulled, keep in mind the most common

mistakes trail-food planners make: taking too much food and things that are too complicated to fix (three-pan main dishes) or that take too long. (Fifteen minutes' stove time is usually a sensible top limit, and none too short when six people are huddled under a tarp in the rain.)

THE MASTER PLAN

A good starting point is a trip calendar that graphically shows how many meals you'll need, as well as special requirements and possibilities.

	Fri.	Sat.	Sun.	Mon.	Tues.	Wed.
breakfast	B	B	B	early B	B	B
on the road		hike all day	move camp	(mtn. climb)	loose a.m.	exploring
car lunch	L	L	L	L	L	L
			same camp		move camp	hike out
camp dinner	D	D	D	D	home

For this trip you'd plan:

5 camp breakfasts (1 early/ quick/easy for the mountain-climbing day, Monday; 1 could be late/leisurely for the unstructured morning, Tuesday)

1 car lunch

5 trail lunches (1 during Monday's climb; 1 around camp Tuesday, could use stove)

5 camp dinners (1 quick/ easy for after Monday's climb)

snacks

drink powders and such

Such a chart makes it less likely you'll forget something—a whole meal or snacks, for instance—or take too much.

Of course, the best-laid plans must always be open to influence by the conditions at hand: weather, how energetic or tired the group feels, how much daylight is left when you reach camp, an abundance of wild huckleberries or trout. Don't let a rigid "Monday dinner" and "Tuesday lunch" schedule trap you into frustrating or inadequate fare. Be free instead to make an on-the-spot decision each mealtime about what's best to eat then. Take advantage of good weather and high energy levels, using the most complicated and longest-cooking foods when those conditions prevail. Then you'll have quick and easy meals in reserve for less favorable times, should they come.

In the process of deciding what foods to pack, *always* measure possibilities against these overall goals:

- The food should be a satisfying part of the fun
- What you take needs to fuel you adequately

Until you get the hang of food planning, it's helpful to look at a trip's rations in terms of calories needed (see pages 4–5) and ideal food weight—2 pounds or less per person per day. These two rules will help you pare down (or build up) individual food items and totals to a reasonable level.

Another tool I still find helpful after many years of wilderness eating is to make brief notes of quantities I take, constantly modifying amounts as I learn through experience.

GUIDELINES

When you've been delegated (or maybe even volunteered!) to plan menus for your group's next wilderness venture, what specific factors influence your planning? At least the following need to be considered:

- length of trip
- type of activity: leisurely? moderate? strenuous?
- probable weather conditions
- availability of water
- stove or open fire
- number of people
- amount of time for cooking
- amount of money to spend
- how much variety is needed
- foods to avoid

LENGTH OF TRIP

Short trips are the time to splurge on shish kebab, fresh-egg omelet, baking in camp. On brief trips you have more room in your pack and can take heavy foods and some that might not keep well beyond a day or two (or might get smashed if hauled around for long). On longer trips you can frequently enjoy the same wonderful dishes simply by making some substitutions for ingredients. (See pages 91–92 for ways to lighten your dinner fare.)

On a hike of several days, plan to use the heaviest and most perishable foods first. For example, you might incorporate fresh veggies in the first main dish or two; have smoked sausage links, homemade muffins and juicy melon chunks for the first or second breakfast; perhaps flour tortillas with meat filling in the third dinner.

If you are planning an extended trip that involves picking up part of your food supply along the way, the legs of the trip may be of unequal length: a four-day stretch, then a food pickup for the next seven-day leg, then a pickup for the last five days. In this kind of planning there is the possibility of more flexible meals, because heavier (and also bulkier) things can be used for the shorter stretches. If someone is meeting you with your food drop (rather than it being cached ahead of time), you can ask them to include some fresh foods, such as fruit, cheese, cookies, meat.

TYPE OF ACTIVITY

If your plans call for a steady output of large amounts of energy, you'll need a substantial diet of edibles that are easily prepared; otherwise there's the temptation to skip fixing a proper meal when you're really exhausted. For instance, a long approach and a mountain climb, or a trek covering 10 to 12 miles a day over rugged terrain won't leave you much pep for elaborate cooking, but you'll need extra nutrition. When you are actually hiking only a few hours out of the day and more time is set aside for camp activities, you can enjoy more food fussing.

PROBABLE WEATHER CONDITIONS

Mild temperatures and dry skies make for comfort around camp, including during the meal preparations. Except when you're bugged by mosquitoes or flies, you will probably enjoy spending more time on food fixing in mild camping weather. If you do much high-elevation hiking, however, mornings and evenings can be surprisingly nippy. You may then want to wait till the rising sun hits camp to fix breakfast, and have dinner before evening coolness takes over.

If it is likely that you'll be cooking in some severe or uncomfortable weather, you'll need to include at least *some* meals that can be prepared very quickly with a minimum of effort. Fingers numb with cold can make the simplest motions seem difficult. This is a time when freeze-dried foods or the quickest of the one-liners (see pages 13 and 82–92) can be appropriate. When weather conditions and a hard day's work have sapped your strength, you *need* a hot, nourishing meal to raise your spirits and ward off hypothermia. With a quick main dish, only a drink and some dried fruit, cookies or candy are needed to make a complete and hearty meal.

And what if a chilly rain or snow is falling in the morning but you need to eat breakfast and break camp? You simply roll over in your sleeping bag, take the "blizzard breakfast" out of your pack, and dine on smoked salmon, homemade granola and dried fruits. *Then,* properly fueled, you can quickly dress, take down the tent and move on.

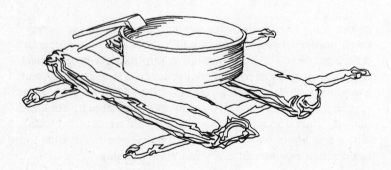

AVAILABILITY OF WATER

On a desert walk, where water is scarce or nonexistent and what you have is what you bring, most of your foods should already contain their moisture. Take brownies rather than instant pudding, canned fruit instead of applesauce mix that must be cooked with water. Choose a main dish that requires little water: a rice-based dish takes less than one with noodles or macaroni, and canned beef with gravy is more appropriate than TVP or freeze-dried meat.

On snow trips, lack of running water can also be an important limitation to consider, because often you'll be using fuel and stove time to melt water before you can even *begin* to cook.

USE OF STOVE OR OPEN FIRE

If you choose to cook on a hiker's stove, you'll need to plan menus that this method can accommodate. For instance, a meal with three parts that need cooking in separate pans (such as split pea soup, beef Stroganoff and a cooked pudding) is hard to do on *one* stove unless you stretch dinner out and eat one course at a time, slowly. You may not even have enough pots! Soup and a one-pot main dish can be cooked in quick succession, without washing the pot in between. If you're using only one stove, there is a lot to be said for no-cook desserts (such as fruit leathers, cookies or a sweet, rich bread) and things that can be mixed right in their carrying bags (such as instant pudding or cheesecake; see "A Bag Is a Bowl!" page 37).

Sometimes wood supplies, weather conditions and the presence of an established fire ring justify a small open fire for cooking. If you're cooking on a campfire, there is probably enough wood available that you don't have to limit your menus to quick-cook foods. When you carry all the fuel you use, more careful planning is needed so that you don't run out. But a small, subdued fire will do a fine job for dishes that may need to simmer 20 minutes or more. Just watch the pot to make sure there's enough liquid and that it is set where the fire isn't too hot.

Cooking on a fire coats pans with soot, so if this is your method, you'll need to carry the blackened pans in a cloth or plastic bag to avoid getting everything else in your pack black too. Some people first coat pan bottoms with soap, making them easier to clean.

You may want to use a simple backpacker's grill, but sizable, firm branches work fine as a platform as long as a pot watcher keeps an eye out for possible tipping pots and readjusts the cooking shelf when needed. Do remember that pots are hot; use a glove or pot grabber (hinged metal device that clamps on the lip, available from the outdoor store).

Some foods are actually easier to do on an open fire: cobbler, biscuits, pancakes, egg dishes. Reflector ovens require open fires. They are fun (if you don't mind carrying an extra 2½ pounds) but not really necessary. Just rig a foil hood over a pie pan or cooking pot so that when you set the pan at one edge of the fire, heat is reflected onto the goodies in it.

NUMBER OF PEOPLE

Traveling alone usually precludes dishes that are easier to make in quantity, such as spaghetti or stew. Some freeze-dried entrees are packaged in one- or two-serving sizes. Many one-serving soup packets are available that can be transformed into filling dinners by the addition of some quick-cooking couscous and cheese.

When planning meals for one or two people, you may want to use more no-cook foods in order to simplify preparation. Or, package enough of just one main dish to do for *all* dinners, and vary its accompaniments. For a four-night snow trip, a friend and I dumped freeze-dried beef Stroganoff from a #10 tin into a 1-gallon ziplock bag. Each night we scooped out a fourth of it to reconstitute for dinner. It was different every time—meaty one night, saucy the next, thicker the next!

For three or more people, a big pot of hearty Bouillabaisse (page 77), Sunset on the Plains (page 76) or Cascade Stewpot (page 80) hits the spot!

No matter whether you're planning for one appetite or ten, the common tendency is to pack too much food. Remember that ingredients such as noodles, rice and dried vegetables swell (even double) as they cook. You'll almost always be safe if you estimate amounts on the conservative side.

AMOUNT OF TIME FOR COOKING

Consider a no-cook or mini-cook trip if weather isn't severe and you want to save time and the weight of stove/fuel/pans. If time is no obstacle, have fun preparing more elaborate meals.

There's an abundance of things that need no in-camp cooking at all. Many can be eaten as is: granola, trail mix, fruit leather, bagels, jerky, peanut butter/molasses spread, zucchini or banana bread, fig bars, sesame wafers and the like. Others just soak in either cold or hot water: many cereals, tabbouli salad, dried-fruit compote. Food can be soaked in a pan, or often right in the bag it traveled in.

AMOUNT OF MONEY TO SPEND

Costs for hiking foods can vary widely. On the high end of the scale is the use of all prepackaged (mainly freeze-dried) foods. The low end of the money scale calls for putting together all your own beverages, cereals, main dishes, snacks and so on. More time is needed for the do-it-yourself route, of course.

HOW MUCH VARIETY IS NEEDED

People differ greatly in how much sameness they can tolerate or enjoy in wilderness meals. For the sake of ease in planning, packaging and preparing, you might sometime elect to plan meals that repeat the same basic main dish several times, but vary it with different spices, sauces or toppings.

If you want to strive for a varied menu, there are several things to keep in mind. Make sure your main dishes use different bases (rice, spaghetti, bulgur, noodles, etc.). Desserts should be of varied textures, not *all* puddings or cookies. Try Four-Minute Fudge (page 95), Traveling Grasshopper Pie (page 95), various trail shakes (page 110), Apple–Peach Crunch (page 97) and so on.

Breakfast is probably the most difficult meal to keep interesting, even at home. Use different types of cooked cereals, adding chopped dried fruits or condensed mincemeat bar. Many of the things we usually consider as snacks are also good for breakfast: supercookies, gorp, pemmican, Mountain Bars (recipes in chapter 12). Choose different kinds of bread (pages 63–65) or English muffins to toast.

FOODS TO AVOID

Check with group members about any foods they can't eat due to allergies. Are any vegetarians? What about strong dislikes or preferences?

LEARN AS YOU EAT

Soon after each trip, take a few minutes to evaluate the food and learn from experience. What did you bring back home? Why? How much more or less should have been taken? Modify cooking techniques that didn't work well, change recipes that sounded good on paper but needed slight alteration to be really tasty or workable. Which foods did you wish for, and which would you like to forget?

I keep notes on such matters in a Trail Foods folder, where I also gather recipes that sound good, ideas from friends, magazine clippings and the like. The folder supplies me with plenty of ideas for future trips and keeps me from repeating the same mistakes.

FOOD TRADE

Even with the best of planning, by the last couple of days of a long hike, people are often getting tired of their lunch and snack foods. The woods ring with deftly arranged swaps—"My fig bars for your meat sticks?" A full-scale food trade livens things up! Spread a poncho on the ground. Then everyone tosses on foods he'd happily bid adieu to and scoops up new, more interesting fare to spark the remaining miles.

4

~~~~~~

Packaging

A s you assemble foods at home, organize them in a way that makes finding and fixing go smoothly in camp. Some people gather all foods together for each day; some like to pack all breakfasts together, all lunches in one bag, dinners in a third. Recycled bread and produce bags serve well for these groupings, as do stuffsacks of different colors.

Prepackage to eliminate bulky materials (that also add weight to your load) and the bother of dealing with separate bags and cartons. Prepackaging also cuts down on the amount of garbage you have to haul home. If you're putting together one-pot main dishes, you'll probably be combining several packages—such as meat or meat substitute, vegetable, sauce or soup mix, rice, and so on—together in one bag.

Reading instructions as you prepackage also leads you mentally through all the steps of preparing the foods you're taking, so that every necessary ingredient and tool gets packed. The slapdash packer who doesn't take this kind of care frequently forgets margarine for the macaroni and cheese, dry milk for the pudding, a can opener for the tuna or oil for cooking the pancakes.

A side benefit of prepackaging is the opportunity to slip added power into your trail fare—extra dry milk in with the amount called for in instant pudding, or a spoonful of wheat germ in the cereal bag.

The packaging system I prefer calls for using different sizes of sturdy, resealable ziplock bags for many things and two kinds of open-once bags for others: (a) tough baby-bottle bags (about 2¢ each, sold in packages of 100); and (b) the boilable bags (because they're sturdy) sold for use with a home bag-sealing machine, such as Seal-A-Meal or Meals-in-Minutes. The last two kinds of bags can be sealed in any size or shape desired.

In addition to ziplock and sealable bags, I recycle other household plastic bags from bread, produce and the like. Clear ones let you see what's inside. Add your own labels to a printed or colored bag you can't see through.

Any bag can have a second life on the trail, holding maps, wet clothes or garbage to pack out. Back home, they can be washed and reused several times.

To close any bag other than ziplock, rubber bands or tape are preferable to wire twistems, which tend to poke holes in nearby things. Before sealing, press out as much air as possible to slow deterioration and reduce bulk.

Organizing my provisions, I package each dinner separately, but my breakfast foods for a trip all ride together in one bag. Often all lunch items are packed in another bag. The lunch foods for a group trip of several days could be divided into two large bags, each holding a variety of foods and carried by two different people.

All bags should be labeled with contents and instructions, in the simplest form possible. Sometimes I write directly on clear bags with indelible felt-tipped pen; sometimes on freezer tape, which adheres well in damp conditions. Labels might read, for instance:

> Lemon pudding + * 1½ c. water
> Drink, 1 qt.

Sometimes labels distinguish look-alikes, such as fruit drink

---

*You will see this + symbol frequently throughout the book; it's my shorthand for "add in."

and fruit gelatin, dry milk and the plaster of Paris packed for making animal-track casts!

Powdered foods and others you'll open once only, and that are not going to be mixed in the bag, can be handily sealed in baby-bottle bags and boilable bags. Trimmed baby-bottle bags are the perfect size to hold drink mix (cheaper bought in bulk and repackaged), main-dish toppings and other foods in small quantities, and they are tougher than sandwich bags. They can be sealed with a home bag sealer. To guard against leaks, make two lines of seal ¼ inch apart. Use a felt-tipped pen to note contents right on the bag.

Seal larger quantities of food in the boilable bags. These are also fine for packing home-cooked entrees such as chili or stew, which can be frozen at home and heated in camp by simply dropping the sealed bag into a pan of boiling water. (Precooked items such as these are heavy, but sometimes suitable for short trips. They are your own thrifty counterpart to retort foods.)

Ziplock bags work very well for powdered or other foods that you'll dip into more than once (such as Russian Tea mix, gorp, candy) or that you'll want to mix in the bag (such as pudding or sour-cream sauce mix). When empty, they can be easily packed out, and there's no mixing bowl to wash. (Please don't burn plastic; the fumes are noxious.)

Pack fragile edibles, such as brownies, on the Styrofoam trays that meat and fish are sold on. Two, banded together face to face, are almost weightless but keep things from getting smashed. Delicate foods you'd like to keep cool (such as Ham—Pineapple Rollups, page 115), also do well packed this way. Wrap the whole bundle in a small towel or sweater for extra insulation.

Plastic cannisters from 35-mm film have good tight lids and are useful for toting small amounts of liquids and powders: spice and herb blends, soy sauce, sherry, sesame seeds, hot mustard, salad dressing and such. You can also buy or recycle small plastic bottles with leakproof tops. Look in the outdoor store and the travel section of the drugstore.

A BAG IS A BOWL!

Goodies that need mixing in camp with cold water can be pre-packaged at home in 1-quart ziplock bags that double as collapsible bowls. Besides saving cleanup, this avoids tying up a pan. Many things, such as dips and cold cereals, can be served right from the bag. Foods you might prepare this way are the following:

- pudding mix packed with instant dry milk
- biscuit/dumpling mix
- trail shake
- dip mix
- pancake batter
- sour-cream sauce mix and instant dry milk
- cobbler topping

For all except pudding and trail shake, add the required amount of water, push out most of the air, seal and then knead the bag with your fingers. Puddings and trail shakes mix best by sealing some air into the bag and then shaking vigorously. Backpackers stand in line for the kneading and shaking privileges!

Other uses for resealable bags: adding cold water to dried fruits and setting aside to rehydrate, thus cutting cooking time for compotes and cobblers; saving leftovers for the next meal; soaking salads such as Lebanese Tabbouli Salad (page 157) or Green and Orange Salad (page 155).

GET IT TOGETHER

In my basic packaging system, all the ingredients for a dish go together in a bag, and all parts of a meal (main dish, dessert, beverage) are grouped together in a larger bag. This larger one can be either a 1-gallon ziplock bag, a recycled bread wrapper or a produce bag.

This system makes locating the food a simple task; a meal is never stalled because one person has half the main dish while the sauce is in another pack, the owner of which is still trudging toward camp.

It's helpful to carry a separate bag that holds things used for more than one meal: salt and pepper, margarine, some beverages, perhaps cheese, cooking oil, dishwashing tools, matches, can opener if you'll need one . . . all the general supplies.

Some travelers like to put this community bag, their eating utensils and their share of the food into a big stuffsack made of water-repellent coated nylon. Then it all stays together in the pack.

For trips of several days or more, your share of the food may overflow the confines of your pack. The problem can be solved in an evening's time for an investment of a few dollars. From urethane-coated nylon and a two-way zipper (both sold at fabric stores) you can sew an extra pouch that will ride on the top of your pack. Six to eight four-person meals can be carried this way, and the pouch collapses as the contents are used. It is virtually weightless.

Here are two more tricks to employ when your pack bursts its seams:

- Tie on the first day's food in a stuffsack or a lightweight daypack.
- An oatmeal box lashed on the outside of your pack will safely carry lots of smashables, such as crackers and cookies (and you may want to tuck in the cheese to go with the crackers). When empty, the box can hold your laundry or other items.

There are many other possible routes to go in packaging, such as using rigid plastic containers (new or recycled), leaving things in their original foil packets for freshness (be sure to pack out every scrap), clipping instructions off the box and tucking them into your smaller package. You may also prefer to pack each person's lunch items for the whole trip in his own bag, or to gather all the breakfast granola for a week into one bag. (The drawback to that is that you have to remember what day it is and how many meals the supply must cover.) The system I've settled on after many years of experimenting seems to meet my needs for clarity, convenience on the trail and sharing the load and responsibilities.

Let's go through a typical day's meals to show how this system works. (These examples use arbitrary measurements for purposes of illustration. If you use any of the ideas, be sure you determine the correct measurements yourself for the quantities you want.)

BREAKFAST

oatmeal with raisins and banana chips
"Smoked" Fish Treats (page 150)
grapefruit juice
Mexican Mocha (page 108)

At Home

1. Put oatmeal, raisins, banana chips, brown sugar and instant dry milk all together into a small bag. Label: "Oatmeal, 1:1 with hot water in cup."
2. Put "Smoked" Fish Treats into a boilable (or baby bottle) bag, push out all the air and seal with a home bag-sealing machine. Or, pack in a doubled sandwich bag, push out all the air, twist the top and seal with a rubber band.
3. Package the amount of juice powder you want in another bag and seal in the same way. Label: "Juice, 1 qt."

4. From your on hand supply, put the right amount of Mexican Mocha into another bag and seal. Label: "Mex. Mocha, + 4 c. hot water."
5. Now put all four of these bags together into a larger bag. Label: "Breakfast." If you want to specify which day it will be eaten, add "day 2."

LUNCH

rye bread, Triscuits
cream cheese
carrot and celery sticks
salami
instant chocolate malt pudding
fruit drink

At Home

1. Put crackers and bread in one bag, sealing tightly.
2. Either leave the cream cheese in its original wrapper or put it into a bottom-filling plastic carrying tube (less than a dollar at outdoor and sporting goods stores).
3. Cut a chunk of salami the size you need and seal it in a bag.
4. Put the needed amount of fruit drink mix into a bag and seal. Label: "Drink, 1 qt."
5. Into a 1-quart ziplock bag put instant pudding mix, 1 tablespoon malted milk powder and enough instant dry milk to reconstitute into the 2 or 3 cups called for in the pudding directions; seal. Label: "Pudding, + 2 (or 3) c. water, shake." At lunch stop, you'll add the water, seal again some air inside, knead and shake until blended and thick.
6. Now put all four of these bags and the cream cheese together into a larger bag, plus cleaned but *uncut* carrots and celery stalks (they travel better uncut and can be trimmed with a pocket knife at lunchtime). Label: "Lunch."

DINNER

minestrone soup
one-liner (noodles/sausage/
    tomato soup mix/celery and
    pepper flakes)
raspberry Danish Dessert
Russian Tea (page 107)

At Home

1. Repackage a powdered minestrone soup mix or leave
   in its original packet. If rebagged, label: "Soup, simmer
   10 mins. in 3 c. water."
2. Put noodles, tomato-soup packet, celery and pepper
   flakes, salt and pepper all together into one bag. Wrap
   a chunk of summer sausage separately, label "Dice &
   add" and put it into the same bag. Label the whole
   thing: "Main dish, simmer till tender in 5 c. water +
   soup mix."
3. Remove Danish Dessert mix package from its box.
   Write on packet: "Pudding, + 2 c. water, simmer till
   thick." You may want to put this paper packet into a
   sandwich bag if you think it might get torn.
4. From your on-hand supply, put the needed amount of
   Russian Tea mix into a bag. Label: "Russ. Tea, makes 4
   c." Or use tea from the general food bag.
5. Now put all four of these dinner parts together into a
   large bag. Label "Dinner."

5

~~~~

Gearing Up

What basic tools do you need for cooking and eating in the quiet places? Will it cost a small fortune to assemble an adequate outfit? Will it weigh a ton?

You can spend a bundle on clever, fancy items—and you may want to put some of these luxury goodies on your Christmas list—but here's all you really need to get started: stove, fuel flask, pans, pot grabber, water bottle, spoon, cup, bowl, tiny can opener, matches, biodegradable suds, scrubber.

Buying everything new and not pinching pennies, you might spend $75 on adequate kitchen gear (half of which would be for a stove). If that seems steep, cheer yourself up by comparing it with the cost of a night in a motel. Investing in trail gear prepays a lot of future vacations!

There are several resourceful ways to trim the price tag: Remove the handles from thrift store pans or make your own set from graduated sizes of cans, attaching wire bale handles. Eat from a margarine container. Use a folded bandana or glove as a potholder. Carry ordinary matches in a plastic bag instead of buying the expensive weatherproof ones (which seem to be hard to light, anyway).

If you frequently travel in a group, use an indelible felt-tipped pen to mark your initials or name on cooking and eating gear . . . you might all own identical pans and cups.

Like *everything* you tuck into your pack, all kitchen equipment should be lightweight, compact, sturdy, easy to use.

STOVE. In most wild places it's getting less and less appropriate to cook over open fires, which sterilize the soil, leave ugly black scars and use up dead wood. Besides, a stove lets you cook anywhere, in any weather, and it doesn't get your pans all sooty.

The most common kinds of one-burner hiker's stoves use either white gas or butane. Butane is packed under pressure in a cannister, and stoves that burn it are easy to operate. Among their drawbacks: Fuel is relatively expensive; they don't work well at low temperatures; heat output decreases as the amount of fuel in the cannister decreases.

For years I've traveled with a common and simple white-gas-burning stove, the Swedish-made Svea 123. With the addition of the Mini-Pump designed to work with a Svea or Optimus, this tidy little burner serves me reliably both summer and winter. It has its idiosyncrasies (every type of stove does), and is not as high-powered as the Coleman Peak 1 or the MSR (Mountain Safety Research) stove. But with its nesting two-piece wind-screen/base, two pans and lid, I've turned out many a memorable meal! White gas costs just pennies an hour to burn.

If your group consists of four or more people and you plan to be out several days (especially in nippy weather), a combination of two stoves will meet your cooking needs well. A high-powered stove with a built-in pump uses more fuel, but very efficiently does quick jobs such as boiling water. To simmer foods that require gentler cooking, a less powerful, more adjustable stove works better.

FUEL FLASK WITH POUR SPOUT. On a weekend trip, most stoves will need refilling a time or two, especially if you're boiling water to purify it. So you need a way to carry extra fuel and some kind of pour spout that lets you transfer it to the stove without spilling. Most convenient is the spout/lid combination that doesn't leak when closed for carrying.

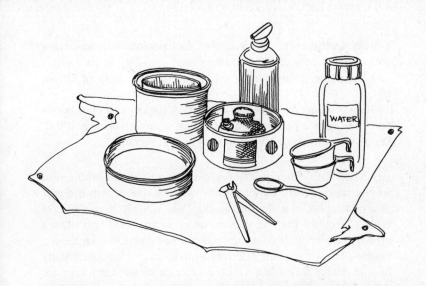

Cylindrical, anodized aluminum flasks are most popular. Be sure yours has a good gasket and is leakproof, and of course never carry food in the same part of your pack. If your fuel flask looks or feels similar to any other containers you carry, *label it!*

With a butane stove, you'll need to carry extra cannisters of fuel and tote the empties out.

PANS. Two are usually enough, and often one will do. You can save weight, bulk and money by using doubled foil for a lid. Some pan sets are specifically designed for use with certain stoves, so the whole outfit packs tidily together. Some hikers keep their pots (especially fire-blackened ones) and stove in a large plastic or cloth bag.

POT GRABBER. Backpacking pans don't usually have attached handles, since that would make them awkward to pack. So you need some way of picking them up without burning your fingers. For a dollar or so you can buy a hinged pot grabber that "bites" the lip of the pan.

WATER BOTTLE. This should be of sturdy plastic, and the cap must seal well. You can save a bit by getting a flimsy look-alike, but you'll pay in the end when it leaks all over the rest of your gear . . . often in the car, before you're even at the trailhead. A

1-quart size fits nicely in an outside pack pocket and encourages you to drink enough. Some hikers carry two pint water bottles and hang one handily from a belt-loop with a strip of Velcro tape.

Tie a bootlace or strong cord around the neck of your bottle and then into an extra loop. Hooking a finger through it will keep you from losing the bottle to a swift stream.

EATING TOOLS. Since just about everything you eat on the trail can be tackled with either fingers or a big spoon, skip the cost of a nesting set of knife/fork/spoon. (You already have a pocket knife.) Likewise the five-part metal mess kit. Food spread in a broad, shallow, metal container cools before it gets to your mouth. Plastic or wood insulates better, as do smaller containers. Many people prefer plastic cups to the broader metal Sierra cups for this reason. I find my two plastic cups with measure marks a handy nesting set of dinnerware that takes up little pack space. Lexan spoons are virtually unbreakable and unmeltable.

CLEANUP STUFF. Usually you'll need just a few paper towels (or a soft old diaper or kitchen towel), a small scrubbing pad and a bit of biodegradable camp suds . . . a few drops for each cleanup time is plenty. If you're traveling where snowbanks linger, you can skip all of this, since snow is a great abrasive!

AND TWO PERSONAL FAVORITES. Two more pieces of kitchen gear have won a place in my heart and pack because they help things run smoothly:

KITCHEN BAG. All food and gear (except stove) ride together in a packcloth duffel bag with a zipper down the top and two small inside pockets. This bag keeps everything organized, handy and out of the weather.

WATERSACK. This cloth bag with carrying handle and rubber spout holds a 3-gallon plastic bladder. One trip to the water source does it, then you can hang the full bag in the kitchen. When empty, it wads up fist-sized and weighs next to nothing. One of my students used a resourcefully recycled substitute: the bladder from a boxed wine dispenser.

COMPANIONS. I hike with friends who won't hit the trail without certain pet culinary items:

- small wire whisk for mixing gravy, sauces and eggs
- large kitchen spoon minus much of its handle
- small tea kettle
- mini-spatula for stir fries and pancakes
- wooden spoon for Teflon-coated pans
- two-foot square of strong nylon net, which does several jobs such as straining pasta, cleaning wild berries

6

~~~~

Backcountry Kitchen Techniques

*S*imple and basic, the backcountry kitchen has no counters, running water, refrigerator, or four-burner stove. But with a little practice, you'll soon feel at home there. You might even come to enjoy the lack of complicating frills. The fact that equipment is limited leads you to do some homework, simplifying and cutting preparation steps before you hit the trail. The more you do at home, the less is left for camp.

LOW-IMPACT COOKING AND EATING

Whatever cooking equipment and methods you choose, *please* be respectful of the environment and leave as little sign of your traveling through as possible. No garbage strewn around or buried, no plastic or cans "hidden" under logs, no living trees or standing dead ones hacked up for firewood or a kitchen table.

Camp and cook at least 200 feet from any water source, and don't wash dishes in one, even with biodegradable suds. Carry out *all* your litter and whatever you can manage of someone else's . . . a small way to say thank you to the land that gives you so much.

It almost goes without saying that cooking over wood fires is getting less and less appropriate as people-demands on the wilderness increase and its resources decrease. If you do use a fire, keep it small, douse it safely and either use a fire ring that's already there or dismantle yours when you go. And please, *no* fires to scar the fragile shores of lovely lakes.

Two ways you can be kind to the land when cooking and eating are less obvious, but *very* helpful:

- Wear soft-soled shoes around camp to lessen your bulldozer effect on the vegetation (my 15-year-old moccasins also feel great to hardworking feet at the end of a day's hiking).
- When you get water, gather a lot in one trip to the source. Either use a collapsible bucket or watersack that holds a couple of gallons or load several water bottles into a daypack or stuffsack. That way you won't beat a path to the water's edge. In a base camp where you're parked for a while, consider collecting water by a different route each time.

NECTAR OF THE GODS

Water is among our most basic needs. You can't run a backcountry kitchen without lots of it, and it must be free of ingredients that make you sick. (A little glacier flour or lichen debris isn't necessarily cause for alarm.)

In most places, sadly, the days of being able to drink untreated water safely are gone. With increased use of our wilderness areas has come a rise in the incidence of intestinal upsets caused by microorganisms in the water. At least one such ailment—giardiasis—is serious and long-lasting enough not to be taken lightly . . . unless you don't mind risking diarrhea that can last for weeks, abdominal cramps, fatigue and weight loss. The only sav-

ing virtue of this disease is its 6- to 15-day incubation period. You'll probably be home by the time it hits.

Can't you tell the water is pure if it *looks* sparkling clean and is aerated as it tumbles over rocks in sunshine? And isn't the water usually safe in remote, less-used areas? Unfortunately, no.

The protozoan bad guy, *Giardia lamblia,* is spread by humans and domestic and wild animals, some of whom may be carriers without showing symptoms. Beavers are frequently blamed for contaminating water sources, hence one nickname for this distressing disease, "beaver fever." But in the wildest backcountry, the feces of an infected deer or marmot near a pristine-appearing creek can be the cause of your discomfort later . . . even miles and months away! Hardy little *Giardia lamblia* can live in cyst form in the coldest of waters for *months,* so untreated water can't really be considered safe even in winter.

I *miss* the lift to spirit and body that used to come with a good creek draught. But the risks have changed my habits, and

I now purify all water for drinking, cooking and brushing teeth. How?

The traditional options have been: chemical treatments (iodine, halazone tablets and such), filters and boiling. Current research indicates that heat is the most reliable killer of *Giardia lamblia,* and that *1 full minute of vigorous boiling* is sufficient. My admittedly unscientific field research bears this out. I lead up to twenty backcountry trips each year (summer and winter, 2 to 7 days each) involving nine people each drinking close to a gallon of boiled water a day. (And I log many other miles on trips alone and with family and friends.) *No one* has gotten giardiasis.

FUEL NEEDS

Fill your stove at home (and always light it to make sure it's in good working order) and carry extra fuel. Estimate generously . . . it's better to bring home unneeded fuel than to run out.

On a trip where one stove serves two or three hikers and you're boiling water to purify it, plan on enough fuel for 2 hours' burning time per day. Here a large-capacity stove like the Coleman Peak 1 or the MSR has the edge over one that burns 40 minutes on a tank. Cooking is smoother (when a stove is empty, it must cool before being refilled), and you won't need to pack a fuel flask for a very short trip.

WHAT IF IT RAINS AT DINNERTIME?

I *never* cook inside a tent, even in bad weather. Here's why:

- A flaring stove could burn gear, or my house, or its inhabitants.
- Steam causes drippy condensation.
- I'm a messy cook.
- Carbon monoxide poisoning is a drag.
- It's too small a kitchen with too low a ceiling.

Instead, I counter wet weather at mealtime by (a) taking lots of quick and no-cook foods; and (b) rigging a small tarp as a kitchen roof. (The latter is a great morale booster in groups. It's friendly—and warmer—under a tarp, and you aren't tempted to rush through the meal. There's also the weather-control aspect! Evidence suggests that rigging a tarp under threatening skies keeps the rain away, whereas confidently taking it down brings on showers!

RUNNING A STOVE

When you use a stove, develop a few habits that make things easy and safe. Locate the kitchen away from general camp traffic and several feet from the nearest tent. Be sure the stove sits level and solidly. Gather all gear and foods first so that there's minimal motion around the stove.

Stoves that burn white gas need *clean* fuel to work right. At home when you transfer fuel from the can you buy it in to your stove and flask, pour it through a filter to trap any impurities. And in the field, take care to exclude all dust, dirt and moisture from fuel and stove.

When filling a stove that burns white gas, leave at least ½ inch of air space in the tank to allow for proper pressure buildup. Close your fuel flask tightly after use and set it several feet away from any open flame (fumes can ignite).

Have a pan of water ready to go on, and cover with a lid or foil to speed the heating process. Use pans that aren't too large for the stove; too much overhang reflects a dangerous amount of heat onto the fuel tank, which can then overheat. Big pans on small stoves also tip easily.

If your stove has a heat shield next to the tank, keep it shiny and clean so it can do its job. If there's a safety valve in the tank cap, routinely point it away from you when you set up to cook. It's a blowtorch when it goes!

Wind will dramatically reduce any stove's efficiency, stretch cooking times and increase fuel consumption. So shield the stove in some way from all but the lightest of breezes. Build a low stone wall (dismantle later) or arrange bodies or packs strategically. If your camp is in the open, you might retreat to a nearby grove of trees to cook.

A wind fence can be rigged by stringing a small tarp or poncho between trees. A smaller, more local windscreen can be made from a piece of foil held in place near the stove with a chopstick or small branch.

It's possible to be overzealous about wind protection, however. Once I watched an exploding stove fly 30 feet across camp! Its owner had set the stove in a homemade windscreen fashioned from a coffee can with a few holes punched in the sides. *Too much* heat was reflected back onto the tank.

Some stoves don't know the meaning of the word *simmer,* making it difficult to cook sauces, cereal and such without burning. If the lowest flame is still too strong, hold the pot a bit away from it for part of the cooking time.

If you use a Svea, Optimus or other stove with a wick, never let it burn completely dry. Turn it off when the fuel runs low, or the wick can scorch and lose some of its fuel-conducting capability. And when you shut down these stoves, blow out any small yellow flame remaining. This practice prevents carbon deposits from building up in the nipple. Another way of gumming up your white-gas-burning stove is to store it for long periods with fuel in the tank.

AFTER-DINNER CHORES

When dinner is through cooking, boil water for dishwashing and top up water bottles for the next day (they'll cool by morning). Bag all garbage, including leftover food; human food isn't good for wild critters. Use biodegradable camp suds for a thorough scrub of the dishes once a day, and rinse well; soap film can cause digestive upsets. Scatter waste water broadly over bare soil, rock or bare forest floor at least 200 feet from any water source.

Early-season hikers can often take advantage of lingering snowbanks at cleanup time, since snow is an excellent scouring agent. Dig down to clean snow, then stir some around in your bowl and pans with a spoon.

PROTECTING THE PANTRY

Backpackers share the wilds with lots of other hungry and resourceful animals, and we can hardly blame them if they occasionally take advantage of easy pickin's. Mice, ravens and their kin are everywhere, on the lookout for food that takes little energy to acquire.

Short of an impractical armored cache box, there's no absolutely critterproof way to carry and store trail food. A mouse is small and agile enough to go almost anywhere he chooses. But you *can* make things a little less likely to be gnawed at.

Some people *never* allow any food in their tents. I do, and have yet to find entry holes nibbled in mine. (My time will no doubt come.) I have, however, wakened to the patter of little feet around the food bag I was using as a pillow in snow camp. But the door zipper was broken, a blatant invitation.

If you leave your pack out at night, take *all* foods out, then leave zippers and flaps unfastened. The odor of food is still there, and curious furry beings can then investigate by going in and out the easy way instead of chewing their way through.

What do you do with food at night or when you're away from camp? Hang it all, including the garbage, which smells good too! Gather supplies in a big heavy-duty trash bag, which both protects from moisture and seals in attractive odors. In a group, it's helpful if each person's food is in a separate stuffsack or daypack.

Rig a sturdy line several feet off the ground between trees and hang the stores from it several feet out from the nearest trunk. A mesh sling or bag gives extra support to a heavy food bag. A mini-caribinier provides a handy way to hang and remove the bag without having to disturb the crossline.

Some folks go one step further. A friend, dismayed at a mouse's piracy of her hanging rations on Mount Rainier, devised a successful deterrent. She poked a hole in the center of an empty tuna can, turned it upside down and ran the line tying up her food bag through it. My personal feeling is that she was lucky only timid, nonaerial mice were abroad that night.

Usually—except in bear country, where *much* more care must be taken—this hanging system affords enough protection. Obviously, any self-respecting mouse or chipmunk who is determined will simply chuckle his way into the feast you've provided. On the rare occasions when that happens, share philosophically.

KEEPING THINGS COOL IN WARM WEATHER

Early in summer, lingering snowbanks can provide refrigeration. Be alert to tunneling and flying thieves, however! Trail companions once completely buried their plastic-bagged goodies in snow near camp. Returning from an afternoon's walk, they found scattered empty bags and telltale raven tracks all over the snow. Most birds aren't known for their acute sense of smell; the clever fellow had obviously watched them bury the food, then helped himself when they were gone.

Lacking snow, a stream or lake can keep things cool. Secure food in leakproof plastic bags under the water. Caution: Anchor it *well,* and be aware that other hungry beings may find your cache irrestible.

If there's no water or snow around, the coolest place is probably deep in your pack, under the shade of a tree.

DON'T HELP A GOOD BEAR GO BAD

Bear country requires special precautions. You'll need to hang all food much higher—ideally, at least 15 feet above the ground, 10 feet from the nearest trunk and 5 feet below the supporting limb. This means you'll need a *long* piece of sturdy line and a way to secure a rock to one end. I load a small stuffsack with one and tie it on. Lob this weighted end over a high limb, then tie your protected food bag in its place. Hoist away, anchor the other line end to another tree and hope that the local bears aren't too savvy.

In bear territory, the food hang, packs and kitchen should be well away from where you sleep. And don't sleep in the clothes you cook in.

COOKING IN VERY COLD
WEATHER OR SNOW

The three-season backpacker's first ventures into winter camping are likely to involve a lot of learning, especially when it comes to planning and preparing food. There's a whole new set of conditions to be worked with, and most of them make food-related tasks trickier, more difficult and more crucial.

It's sometimes possible to get along using the same equipment, techniques and menus that work in mild weather. More often, relying on them can make for frustration and disgruntled campers. At its worst, this approach can pave the way for very serious problems, since the winter wilderness is not nearly as forgiving of mistakes.

Because winter camp cooking is really a specialized form of the art, and because increasing numbers of backpackers are heading for the wilds in winter, I've devoted an entire chapter to the challenges of eating well in the snow (see "Winter Camp Cookery," beginning on page 159).

7

~~~~~

Starting the Day

*E*ven if you're a light- or no-breakfast person at home, in the wilds you'll need to be kind to your body with an initial fueling of some sort. There are lots of good things that will do the job besides the traditional cereal, eggs and bacon. How about a cup of Hot Malt (page 109), some Sherpa Tea (page 108), home-brewed Instant Breakfast Drink (page 129), smoked fish (page 150), fruit leather (page 151)... or, for a quick, nourishing no-cook start to a mountain-climbing day, Trail Shakes (page 110) and Peanut Butter Supercookies (page 102)? A perusal of the snack foods list (see chapter 12) shows that many of these high-energy items will double well for breakfast.

If your travels take you out in very wet or cold weather, you should deliberately plan a few "blizzard breakfasts." These can be eaten *before* you stir out of your sleeping bag and begin to lose precious body heat. The savings in terms of comfort and efficiency are worth a few crumbs in the bed.

Blizzard Breakfast #1	Blizzard Breakfast #2
smoked salmon (page 150)	turkey jerky (page 149)
mixed dried fruits	fruit leather (page 151)
Probars (page 59)	Pumpkin Bread (page 63)

The grocery store list found in Chapter 2 is divided into separate meals, and you'll find many breakfast possibilities there. Here are some other ideas to consider:

- Fortify cooked cereals with wheat germ, chopped nuts, sunflower seed kernels and such, which are added at home when you package the cereal. At that time, also add instant dry milk and brown, white, or date sugar. Combining it all makes for less fuss, and it always stays warm. Just use a little more water when mixing in your bowl or cooking.
- Package raisins or finely chopped dried fruit such as apricots, apples, peaches or pears along with cereal.
- In camp, add a blob of peanut butter to hot cereal for an exciting taste and a shot of protein.
- Use fruit leathers as is or torn into muffin-sized pieces that double as jam on your toast.
- Make fruit sauce by stewing any combination of dried fruits in water to cover for a few minutes, sweetening with a little honey if you like. The smaller the pieces, the shorter the cooking time. Good as is, or poured over granola in your bowl.
- Pancakes are a bit tricky to fix on a hiking stove, but sometimes fun and worth the effort. Remember to pack cooking oil, frying pan and pancake turner. Instead of filling the pan with tiny pancakes, try one large one, which can then be divided. Keep 'em coming! Carry and mix pancake batter in a 1-quart ziplock bag.
- Cook thinnish batter for cornbread, coffee cake or muffin mix in pancake form.
- Add fresh or rehydrated dried berries, cooked sausage, bacon bits, peanut butter or crumbled dried banana chips to pancake batter.

- Melt margarine right along with the syrup as you make or heat it (otherwise it's hard to spread on those pancakes in the chill mountain air).
- Top pancakes with stewed fruit, applesauce or jam.
- Sandwich two pancakes around a layer or two of fruit leather.

SOME MORE BREAKFAST THINGS YOU CAN MAKE OR PREPACKAGE AT HOME

Sunrise Spuds

An easy, pleasant change from cereal and such, especially welcome midway on a long trip.

At home, bag together (for each hefty serving): ½ cup instant potato flakes, 1 tablespoon instant dry milk, 1 teaspoon Butter Buds, salt and pepper to taste. In a separate bag, pack a handful of precooked, crumbled bacon (or plan to use chunks of salami from your lunch supply). *In camp:* Put all the ingredients in your bowl (along with a few bits of cheese if you like) and pour in ½ cup boiling water. Stir and enjoy.

Rice Pudding

At home, bag together (for each serving): ½ cup quick rice, a handful of raisins or dried apricot bits, sweetening if desired, a dash of cinnamon, and ¼ cup instant dry milk. *In camp:* Cook gently in 1½ cups water for 6 to 8 minutes.

Probars

Your own high-protein breakfast bars are chewy and substantial, giving you energy for the morning with no in-camp cooking needed. This recipe makes about 12 bars; wrap and freeze what you don't need for your first hike.
Preheat oven to 350°F. Beat together until thick:

3 eggs

⅓ cup honey

Then blend in:

5 tablespoons whole wheat
   flour
½ cup *each* ground sesame
   seeds and ground sunflower
   seed kernels

1 cup chopped nuts
1 cup toasted wheat germ
1 cup sweetened coconut
   flakes

Press firmly into a greased 8-inch square pan and bake for 25 minutes, or until lightly brown. Cut into 12 bars, then let cool.

Granola Crunchers

No preservatives or artificial anything in your homemade bars! A batch of 12, with some for the freezer.

½ cup each:
softened margarine
honey
brown sugar, packed

½ teaspoon vanilla extract
5 cups granola (look for
bargains in bulk at large grocery outlets or natural foods
   stores)

Preheat oven to 400°F. Combine all ingredients and firmly press the mixture into a greased 9-by-14-inch pan. Bake for about 20 minutes, or until lightly browned and bubbly. Let cool partially, then cut into bars.

Grandola Bars

Less chewy, more like a bar cookie.

½ cup margarine
1¾ cups brown sugar, packed
1 egg
1 teaspooon vanilla extract
1½ cups whole wheat flour

1½ teaspoons baking powder
1 teaspoon salt
1½ cups granola
1½ chopped nuts

Preheat oven to 350 ° F. Melt margarine, then remove from heat and stir in sugar, then egg and vanilla. Mix flour, baking powder and salt, Gently blend in (don't beat) sugar mixture, then granola and nuts. Spread in a greased 9-by-14-inch pan. Bake for 25 minutes. Makes 12 bars.

Protein-Power Cereal

has a delightfully different peanutty flavor and can be eaten either cold or can be cooked for a couple of minutes. For 3 servings,

Bag together:

1 cup quick oatmeal
⅓ cup toasted wheat germ
⅓ cup chopped roasted peanuts
¼ cup each: raisins, chopped dried apples or apricots, sunflower seed kernels

½ cup instant dry milk
1 tablespoon date sugar

In camp: Either add 1½ cups cold water, mix and eat OR add mix to 2 cups boiling water, stir and simmer gently for 2 minutes.

Sesame–Raisin Wakeup

(ABOUT 8 SERVINGS)

At home, combine:

1 cup toasted sesame seeds
¼ cup each: sunflower seed kernels, bran flakes, chopped nuts

½ cup each: flaked coconut, raisins, toasted wheat germ
1 cup instant dry milk
1 teaspoon ground cinnamon

Pack ½ cup mix for each serving. *In camp:* Put ½ cup mix in bowl, stir in ½ cup cold or hot water.

Mountain Cereal

(MAKES ABOUT 24 SERVINGS)

In a large bowl, mix together:

4½ cups quick oatmeal
1½ cups pumpkin seeds, chopped

2 cups sunflower seed kernels
1 cup shredded coconut
¼ cup sesame seeds, ground

In a separate bowl, blend together:

½ cup warm water
¾ cup honey

¼ cup vegetable oil
1 teaspoon salt

Mix all ingredients well and bake at 275°F, stirring often, until golden brown (about 10 minutes). Now add:

2 cups raisins

½ cup dried banana chips, crumbled

Stir often as mixture cools. Store in sealed bags in the refrigerator.

Granola

Preheat oven to 300°F. Mix together:

2 cups quick oatmeal
1 cup sesame seeds
1 cup rye flakes
1 cup roasted soybeans
½ cup pumpkin seeds
1 cup sunflower seed kernels

1 cup toasted wheat germ
½ cup broken cashews
½ cup broken pecans
1 cup slivered almonds
½ cup shredded coconut

Add:

½ cup vegetable oil
¼ cup honey

¼ cup molasses

Use hands to mix well. Spread on shallow pans not more than ½ inch thick. Bake for 15 minutes. Stir; bake for 5 to 10 minutes longer, watching carefully that it doesn't burn. Sprinkle over the top: raisins, chopped dried apricots, chopped dates to taste. Store in tightly closed plastic bags in the refrigerator.

Spotted Applesauce

(SERVES 4)

At home, bag together:

2 cups chopped dried apples
½ cup brown sugar
½ cup raisins

1 teaspoon ground cinnamon
½ teaspoon ground nutmeg

In a separate bag, pack ½ cup chopped roasted peanuts. *In camp:* Either soak overnight in water to cover OR simmer until tender (5 minutes or so) in water to cover. Top each portion with chopped nuts, for extra protein and a taste treat.

BREADS FOR BREAKFAST
AND LATER

Dense, moist breads are a versatile treat on the trail, and a natural for easy breakfasts. When I make any of these favorites at home before a trip, I bake some of the batter in the form of muffins and the rest in mini loaf pans, tidy bundles that are easy to pack. If pack space is tight, remember that bread takes less room than muffins. Besides tasting terrific in the morning, substantial breads are a sweet addition to lunch or a fine dessert with dinner. Each of these breads is rich and flavorful and needs no spread to be palatable. Because they're moist, they'll taste fresh for several days.

Pumpkin Bread

(MAKES 3 STANDARD LOAVES)

5 cups sifted whole wheat flour
4 cups sugar
3 cups cooked pumpkin
2 cups chopped walnuts

1 cup vegetable oil
1 teaspoon salt
1 tablespoon pumpkin pie spice
4 teaspoons baking soda

Preheat oven to 350°F. Mix all ingredients in a large bowl and divide among 3 greased loaf pans. Bake for 1 hour and 10 minutes.

Zucchini Bread

(2 STANDARD LOAVES)

Preheat oven to 350°F. Combine:

3 cups whole wheat flour
1 tablespoon ground cinnamon
1 teaspoon baking soda

1 teaspoon salt
1 teaspoon ground cloves
1 teaspoon gound nutmeg

Add:

2 cups grated and drained zucchini

1 cup chopped walnuts

Beat:

3 eggs	1 tablespoon vanilla extract
1½ cups sugar	1 teaspoon grated orange peel
1 cup vegetable oil	

Mix everything together and pour into 2 greased loaf pans. Bake for 1 hour.

Cranberry Coffee Bread
(2 STANDARD LOAVES)

Preheat oven to 350°F. Sift together:

4 cups unbleached white flour	2 teaspoons salt
2 cups sugar	1 teaspoon baking soda
1 tablespoon baking powder	

In a measuring cup put 1 cup orange juice and ¼ cup each of boiling water and melted shortening, and combine with 2 well-beaten eggs. Stir into dry ingredients just until moist. Fold in 3 cups chopped cranberries (run them, partially frozen, through your food grinder) plus ½ teaspoon grated orange peel. Bake in greased loaf pans for 1 hour.

Sweet Wheat and Raisin Bread
(3 STANDARD LOAVES)

Preheat oven to 375°F. Combine:

8 cups whole wheat flour	2 teaspoons salt
4 tablespoons baking soda	

Beat together:

¾ cup vegetable oil	4 cups milk
4 eggs	1 cup honey

Add dry ingredients to beaten mixture, stirring gently just enough to moisten. Stir in:

1¼ cups raisins
⅔ cup coarsely chopped nuts

Spoon into greased loaf pans and bake for about 50 minutes.

Spicy Apple Breakfast Bread

(1 STANDARD LOAF)

2 eggs	1¼ cups whole wheat flour
¼ cup margarine, softened	¼ cup soy flour
⅓ cup honey	1½ teaspoons baking powder
1¼ cups milk	¾ teaspoon baking soda
1 cup uncooked quick oatmeal	2 teaspoons ground cinnamon
1 cup bran cereal	1 teaspoon ground allspice
1½ cups chopped unpeeled apple	1 teaspoon ground nutmeg
	½ teaspoon salt

Preheat oven to 375°F. In a bowl combine eggs, margarine, honey, milk, oatmeal and bran cereal. Stir in chopped apple. In another bowl combine remaining ingredients. Add to first mixture and stir gently just until moistened. Spoon into a greased loaf pan and bake for about 40 minutes.

PACK YOUR CHICKEN

On leisurely mornings you may want to concoct an egg dish for breakfast. Use either fresh eggs (carried in protective plastic cartons, which come in various sizes, or broken into a plastic bottle and buried in your pack to stay cool), or the powdered egg mix available at outdoor stores. Two dry mixes I find palatable are Wakefield Egg Mix and Mountain House Omelets. All three of the following recipes work well as is, topping an English muffin, or spooned into pocket bread.

Herb-Scrambled Eggs

Combine scrambled egg mix with bits of freeze-dried ham, ham-flavored TVP, or jerky torn into small pieces. Stir in the amount of water called for, add a mixture of dried parsley flakes, marjoram, basil and thyme, and let stand a few minutes. Cook in an oiled pan.

Cheese Omelette

Combine scrambled egg mix with a little toasted wheat germ, a dash of garlic powder and the required amount of water. Let stand a few minutes. Cook gently in an oiled pan until the top begins to get firm. Lay sliced cheese on half and fold the egg over. Heat just long enough to melt the cheese.

Bacon Scramble

Precook, crumble and bag some bacon at home. In camp, add it to egg mix with the required amount of water. Let stand a few minutes, then cook in an oiled pan.

8

~~~~~

*Lunch
Is Often
Plural*

*B*ecause of a backpacker's energy needs, it is usually realistic to think of "lunch" as a meal that happens more than once. Some people find that two smaller meals, called "early lunch" and "late lunch," better describe their pattern, or even "constant lunch" to denote the nonstop nibbling that can fill the space between breakfast and dinner. When energy output is high and constant, it makes much better sense to eat small meals more often than three relatively heavy meals a day.

Consult the grocery store foods list (chapter 2) and the section on snacks (chapter 12) for many specific lunch items. On the first day of your trek, consider using fresh and heavier foods such as fruit, hard-boiled eggs, pickles and sandwiches made with regular or pocket bread with meat or fish filling and alfalfa sprouts. In hot weather, be wary of carrying foods containing mayonnaise, however.

Choose sturdy, compact breads or crackers, and top with cheese or a spread. Forms of bread that travel well are: pocket bread, bagels, English muffins, pumpernickel, French bread, small individual loaves, soft or medium-hard rolls, soft bread sticks (make your own).

Try these tough and protein-packed homemade crackers, so sturdy you can sleep on them!

Indestructible Cornmeal Rounds

(MAKES ABOUT 2 DOZEN)

1½ cups cornmeal
¼ cup each:
   sunflower seed kernels
   grated Parmesan cheese
   soy flour
   toasted wheat germ
   sesame meal

2 teaspoons salt
2 tablespoons vegetable oil
1 cup plus 1 tablespoon water

Preheat oven to 350°F and generously oil 2 cookie pans. Mix dry ingredients together. Bring water and oil to a boil, then add to the dry mixture. On a board sprinkled with flour or cornmeal, pat and roll dough to ¼ inch thickness. Cut rounds with a cookie cutter or small frozen-juice can and carefully place them on the pans. Bake for 15 minutes, or until crisp and brown on the undersides, then turn the rounds over and bake until the other side browns. Store in the refrigerator or freezer until your hike.

Zippy Herbed Crackers

(MAKES 24)

Preheat oven to 400°F. Mix together:

2 cups quick oatmeal
¾ cup whole wheat flour
¼ cup toasted wheat germ
¼ cup sesame seeds

½ teaspoon dried oregano
1 teaspoon dried thyme
1 teaspoon salt
½ teaspoon onion powder

Beat together with a fork:

3 eggs
1 tablespoon honey
⅓ cup vegetable oil

Stir into oatmeal mixture with a fork until all dry ingredients are moist. With your fingers, press dough firmly and evenly into an ungreased 9-by-14-inch pan. Bake for 20 minutes, or until golden. Cut into rectangles, let cool on a rack. Store in the refrigerator or freezer until your hike.

The driest *cheeses* keep longest on the trail: Parmesan, Romano, Kasseri, provolone. Intermediate keepers are: Cheddar, Swiss, Edam. Moist cheeses have the shortest pack life: blue, Monterey Jack, Cuminost, Danish.

Some good travelers among the *sausage* family are: dry salami, Landjager, pepperoni and Thuringer. Ask your deli or meat market for other suggestions.

Peanut Butter Spread (page 132) has even more nutritional power than plain peanut butter. For variety, top it with a few dried banana chips, some raisins or other dried fruit bits.

Peppy Margarine

is blended at home and packed into an open-bottomed plastic tube: Soften margarine and blend in chopped fresh or dried parsley, basil and celery seed to taste. Spread on bread or crackers. Any leftovers can go into a soup, main dish or breakfast eggs.

Ham-and-Cheese-Filled Biscuits

are a make-ahead "sandwich" that travels well. Essentially, each serving is made of two big hearty biscuits sealed around a treasure of ham and cheese.

Prepare 2-inch squares of ham and cheese (one for each pair of biscuits). Preheat oven to 400°F. Make a nutritious biscuit dough—either your own favorite recipe or this suggestion. Mix in a large bowl:

2 cups whole wheat flour	1½ teaspoons baking powder
1 cup unbleached white flour	1 teaspoon dried herbs (try
¼ cup soy flour	oregano, basil, parsley)
1 teaspoon salt	1 teaspoon dried minced onion

With a pastry blender, cut in ½ cup margarine. Then stir in 1 cup milk. Roll or pat dough ⅓ inch thick on a floured surface, cut rounds with a biscuit cutter. Spread margarine on all rounds and top half of them with a slice each of ham and cheese.

Using the remaining rounds, put a "lid" on each and squeeze-seal the edges together carefully, wetting with a dab of water as needed to assure no unsealed spots. Bake the filled biscuits on a greased pan for 15 minutes, or until lightly browned. Let cool before wrapping in foil, and refrigerate until your hike.

Most lunch food doesn't require a cooking stove or fire, but on cool days, soup or tea provides a pick-me-up for lagging spirits. And a restful break will let you get a second wind that will make the rest of the day's trek more pleasurable. If you decide on a lunch break that includes cooking, how about...

SUPER SOUPS

Quick Curried Soup

This unusual mix costs just pennies more than the instant soups it builds on and provides more protein.
At home, for 2 servings, bag together:

1 single-serving packet instant green pea soup	⅓ cup instant dry milk
1 single-serving packet instant tomato soup	½ teaspoon curry powder (more for those who like it hot!)

In camp: Divide the mix between two cups, fill with boiling water and stir well.

This blend can be turned into a filling main dish in a jiffy. Add it to 1¼ cups hot water, then stir in an undrained 6½-ounce can of either tiny shrimp or minced clams. Heat through.

Experiment with other soup combinations, always using the opportunity to boost your protein intake with some added instant dry milk.

Hearty Soup Pot

Cook several kinds of soup mix together, adding slivered cheese and crumbled meat or bacon bar. Use plenty of water so that it isn't too concentrated and salty.

Cheese Soup

(SERVES 4)

At home, bag together:

¼ cup each dried carrots, celery, peppers, onion

2 chicken bouillon cubes

In another bag put:

1 cup sunflower seed kernels

⅓ cup instant dry milk

Include in your supplies enough cheese to make 1½ cups grated. *In camp:* Simmer contents of first bag for 15 minutes in 5 cups water, then add second bag plus ¼ cup margarine and 1½ cups grated cheese. Heat till cheese is melted.

Vigorous Veggie Soup

(SERVES 4)

At home, bag together:

½ cup each dried potatoes and carrots
¼ cup each dried celery and onion

2 cubes chicken bouillon
seasonings to taste: marjoram, paprika, caraway seed, dill seed, salt, pepper

In camp: Simmer for 15 minutes in 5 cups water, adding ¼ cup margarine and ½ cup dry milk toward the end.

Fish Chowder

(SERVES 4)

At home, bag together:

½ cup each dried tomatoes and
potatoes
¼ cup each dried onion and
celery

1 teaspoon soy bacon bits
½ teaspoon salt
pepper

Pack separately:

one 6½-ounce can minced
clams

½ cup instant dry milk

In camp: Cook for 10 minutes in 4 cups water. Add undrained clams and dry milk. Cook for 5 minutes more.

Sometimes, because of hot weather, low energy level or the beautiful stream you reach just at lunchtime, the right thing seems to be to have a *long* stop . . . perhaps 2 or 3 hours. Eat the day's largest meal (one-liners serve well here; see chapter 10), doze in the shade, take a dip in the cooling waters, perhaps clean up a bit. Refreshed, resume your hiking midafternoon and travel later into the evening (in summer, evening is a lovely time to walk). Then you eat just a light meal before bed with no need to set up a kitchen. You are even free to choose a campsite without a close water supply.

9

~~~~~

Dinner Fare

*D*inners are usually built around a relatively simple one-pot main dish, with perhaps a hot bread and a dessert. In chapter 10, "The One-Liner," you'll find suggestions for many quick one-pot dinners. Occasionally you may want a more complex dish. This chapter contains some of my favorites.

Most dinner dishes feature a protein—meat or meat substitute. There are several inexpensive sources of main-dish protein available:

- precooked meats from home (page 133)
- small cans of tuna, chicken, turkey
- the addition of nuts, cheese, instant dry milk, sunflower seed kernels, sesame seeds
- combinations such as: bulgur and soy grits (see Berley Lakes Bulgur, page 131); rice, milk, cheese and nuts (see Cashew Rice Curry, page 77)

- Textured vegetable protein (a compact, nourishing, nonperishable boon to backpackers. Two cautions: combine its bland flavor with strong-flavored ingredients; avoid a crunchy or fibrous texture by either cooking in liquid for several minutes or soaking for 6 to 8 minutes before cooking. The granular form gets tender much faster than the chunk form.)

Some protein-rich foods available in freeze-dried form (such as shrimp and meatballs) are occasionally worth the high cost for the variety they make possible.

The taste appeal of freeze-dried main dishes and boxed ones from the grocery store can be improved considerably by the addition of a little margarine and a sprinkling of spices.

To round out a main dish nicely, add . . .

Biscuits or Dumplings
(SERVES 4)

At home, blend, then pack together in a 1-quart ziplock bag:

2 cups baking mix	¼ cup margarine
⅓ cup instant dry milk	

For variety, add any of the following to taste:

grated cheese	soy bacon bits
dried parsley or onion	

In camp: Add enough water to make a stiff dough; seal the bag and mix well.

FOR DUMPLINGS: Open one end of the bag or snip a corner, squeeze golfball-sized dollops of dough directly into your pot of hot soup or stew. Cover and cook for 8 to 10 minutes more, or until the dumplings are dry inside. Dumplings in a thick, rich soup turn it into a filling main dish.

FOR BISCUITS: Have the dough a little dryer; form small patties, cook in a reflector oven or in an oiled frying pan over very low heat, turning once.

Pan Biscuits

are a bit richer. If you have two stoves, fix them while the main dish cooks. If not, cook them first, then keep warm in a lid or foil over the stew as it bubbles.

At home, blend, then pack together in a 1-quart ziplock bag:

1½ cups whole wheat flour
2 tablespoons brown sugar
2 teaspoons baking powder

½ teaspoon salt
⅓ cup instant dry milk
¼ cup margarine

In camp: Add enough water to make a stiff dough; seal the bag and knead well. Shape into small patties. Cook gently in an oiled pan over the low heat for about 8 minutes. When browned on the bottom, turn and brown on the other side.

Pocket Bread (Pita)

makes a fun and hassle-free container for any nonrunny main dish.

Now for a few favorite recipes.

Cheesy Bacospuds

(4 HEARTY SERVINGS)

For those times when you need a hot dinner that's ultralight (8 ounces for 4 servings) and ultraquick (boil the water, and a minute later you're digging in).

At home, bag together:

1½ cups instant potato flakes
⅓ cup instant dry milk
1 packet Butter Buds
1 tablespoon dried parsley flakes
1 tablespoon dried onions or leeks
½ teaspoon salt
pepper

1 package powdered cheese spread (or use cubed fresh cheese from the general supply)
½ cup bacon-flavored textured vegetable protein (bacon bits) OR ½ pound bacon, precooked, crumbled and wrapped separately

In camp: Bring 3 cups water to a boil. Add *all* ingredients; stir and let sit a minute. Then stir to fluff, adding more hot water if too dry.

Sunset on the Plains

(SERVES 3 OR 4)

At home, bag separately:

2 cups pasta (ramen noodles are quickest)

a big handful of dried tomato slices

1 teaspoon mixed dried spices (chili powder, oregano, cumin, etc.)

½ to 1 cup grated or slivered Parmesan cheese

In camp: Cook pasta in 4 cups water until almost tender. Drain most of the water off; spread tomato slices on top. Sprinkle with spices. Cover and cook gently for about 2 minutes, then add cheese. Cover and heat just until cheese melts.

Koosah (Sky) Mountain Stew

(2 BIG SERVINGS)

Try the basic recipe first, or put together variations that are cheaper, lighter or quicker to suit the needs of your particular journey. Adaptations follow the recipe.

At home, pack in a 1-quart ziplock bag:

1 packet sour-cream sauce mix

¼ cup instant dry milk

¼ cup grated Parmesan cheese

¼ teaspoon paprika

Also pack:

1 large clean but unpeeled potato

one 6¾-ounce can boned turkey

one 2-serving package freeze-dried green beans OR 2 handfuls fresh green beans

In camp: Cut the clean, unpeeled potato into small dice and cook it and the green beans for about 8 minutes in 2½ cups boiling water. While this simmers, add ½ cup cold water to the sour-cream sauce bag, seal and knead until well mixed. In the can, cut the turkey into bite-sized pieces. When the veggies are tender, add the sauce mix and turkey, stir well and heat through.

A cheaper and lighter version of this stew can be made by substituting ⅓ cup chicken-flavored TVP for the canned turkey. Increase the water to 3½ cups and rehydrate the TVP with the vegetables as they cook.

If cooking time needs to be shortened, substitute a 3-ounce package of ramen noodles for the potato and 2 thinly sliced fresh carrots for the green beans. These will cook in about 3 minutes.

Cashew Rice Curry
(SERVES 4)

At home, wrap 1 teaspoon salt and 3 teaspoons curry powder in a separate packet.
Also pack:

2 cups quick rice
½ cup instant dry milk
½ cup cashew pieces

3 ounces Havarti or Jack cheese, grated (about ¾ cup)

In camp: Mix the salt and curry powder with a little water to make a paste. Add 4 cups water, mix well and bring to a boil. Stir in rice, cover and simmer gently until soft. Blend in dry milk, then add nuts and cheese. Serve when cheese has melted.

Bouillabaisse
(SERVES 4)

At home, pack:

1 package Knorr Mix for Bouillabaisse
one 4¼-ounce can small shrimp

one 6½-ounce can minced clams

In camp: Heat 4 cups water, stir in bouillabaisse mix. Bring to a boil, then add shrimp and clams and their liquid. Simmer for 12 minutes. Serve with thick chunks of French bread (great for dunking!).

Rice and Vegetable Dinner Mix

(SERVES 4 TO 6)

At home, bag together:

½ cup dried onion
½ cup dried carrots
¼ cup dried parsley flakes

1¼ cups quick brown rice
3 cubes beef bouillon
pepper

Wrap separately:

¼ pound Cheddar cheese

In camp: Bring all but cheese to a boil in 3 cups water, and simmer until tender (12 minutes or more). Top with slivered cheese. Serve when cheese has melted.

Trail Taters au Gratin

(2 HEFTY SERVINGS)

At home, pack:

2 clean but unpared medium
  potatoes
1 medium onion
1 tablespoon dried parsley
  flakes
salt and pepper

½ cup croutons or dried
  coarse bread crumbs
2 ounces Swiss or Cheddar
  cheese
vegetable oil

In camp: Slice potatoes ¼ inch thick into an oiled pan and cook slowly until browned on the bottom. Turn slices over and top with sliced onion. Sprinkle with parsley, salt and pepper and ½ cup water. Cover and cook gently until tender. Spread croutons and slivered cheese over all, cover and remove from heat. Let sit until cheese melts.

Super Scramble

This dish can double as a leisure-day breakfast.
At home, bag together:

2 cups dried potato shreds
½ meat or bacon bar
1 tablespoon dried chopped
  onion

1 teaspoon dried pepper flakes
1 teaspoon dried parsley flakes

Also pack a large chunk of cheese (3 ounces or so). *In camp:* Soak all but the cheese in water to cover for 20 minutes. Drain and cook in an oiled pan until browned. Stir in cubed cheese and heat until melted.

Shrimp Creole

(SERVES 3 TO 4)

At home, pack together:

½ cup dried tomato pieces
¼ cup dried green pepper
   flakes

1 cup quick rice
½ teaspoon salt
pepper

Also pack:

one 4½-ounce can small
   shrimp

1 single-serving packet cream-
   of-mushroom-soup mix

In camp: Cook contents of bag for about 6 minutes in 4 cups water. Stir in soup mix to blend, then add undrained shrimp and more water if needed. Heat through.

Chicken Ragout

(SERVES 4)

At home, bag together:

1 cup dried sliced carrots
½ cup dried sliced celery
½ cup dried sliced potato
¼ cup dried sliced mushrooms
¼ cup dried sliced olives
¼ cup dried chopped onion
1 tablespoon dried parsley
   flakes

1 cup freeze-dried peas
3 cubes chicken bouillon
¾ cup chunked chicken TVP
   (OR 2 small cans boned
   chicken added toward the
   end of cooking time)
a pinch or 2 of anise seed
pepper

In camp: Simmer all ingredients in 6 cups water until tender, 12 to 15 minutes. You may need to add more water as the foods rehydrate.

Wild Goulash

(SERVES 4)

At home, pack:

1 package Knorr mix for
  Goulash
2 cups diced cooked beef
  from home (leftover round
  steak, roast or precooked
  hamburger)

3 cups uncooked noodles

In camp: Stir goulash mix into 2 cups cold water. Bring to a
boil; simmer for 10 minutes, then add meat. Cover and set aside
while you cook noodles in 6 cups water until barely tender.
Drain noodles, then add sauce along with meat and heat through.

Spanish Rice with Meatballs

(SERVES 4)

At home, pack:

1 cup dried tomato pieces
2 tablespoons dried chopped
  onion
4 servings freeze-dried or
  canned meatballs

½ teaspoon salt
pepper
1 cup quick rice
1 packet brown gravy mix

In camp: Cook all but rice for 5 minutes in 3½ cups water. Add
rice, cover and cook for 8 minutes longer. Stir in brown gravy
mix and a bit more water if needed.

Cascade Stewpot

(SERVES 4)

At home, bag together:

½ cup dried diced potatoes
½ cup dried tomato pieces
½ cup dried sliced carrots
1 tablespoon dried chopped
  onion

1 tablespoon dried sliced
  celery
2 cubes beef bouillon

Also pack:

½ cup instant potato flakes   2 cups leftover roast beef OR 1
                                                can roast beef chunks with
                                                gravy

In camp: Cook all but potato flakes and beef for 10 minutes in
4½ cups water. Stir in potato flakes and beef and heat through.

LAST SUPPERS

Toward the end of longish hikes, you hear some connivingly
generous food talk. Rummaging through uneaten items (especially the heavy ones) that have to be hauled out, hikers wax
inventive, resourceful and willing to try any weird combination.
This is the backcountry equivalent to cleaning out the refrigerator.

Carrot and celery sticks that everyone's bored with take on
new life in a sauté. Too-generous amounts of (dry) pasta or rice
find themselves smothered in a unique sauce.

Bonnie's Faute de Mieux

(LITERALLY, "FOR LACK OF SOMETHING BETTER")

Top cooked pasta with a sauce made of melted cheese, a bit of
margarine and diced avocado and cucumber.

Last-Leg Sauté

Sauté bite-sized chunks of all the remaining fresh (maybe slightly
droopy by now?) veggies—carrots, zucchini, celery, yellow summer squash, green beans—in margarine. Toss in slivers of salami.

10

⌘

The One-Liner

No joke... these one-pot main dishes
make the core of either lunch or dinner

The one-liner is simply a pared-down recipe listing only its ingredients, with no instructions or specific amounts included. Baffling? Inadequate? No! Not after you familiarize yourself with this streamlined, creative approach to wilderness feasting. Feasting it is, too. Imagine, for instance, dining on Mount Washington Tuna Curry as the sun sets on your camp:

---

tuna · quick rice · dried peas · curry
sauce · almonds · shredded coconut

To build a one-liner, you start with a basic list of ingredients:

- meats or meat substitutes
- pastas or grains
- vegetables

- sauces
- seasonings
- toppings

Entries in each category are mostly items available at any grocery store. A few will be found in natural foods stores, delis or meat markets, ethnic markets and import stores. Freeze-dried single ingredients like meat or vegetables are sold at outdoor and sporting goods stores. (See chapter 2 for extensive lists of foods from many sources.) If you venture into home drying, you'll be able to add even more possibilities to your lists of ingredients.

The one-liner omits amounts of each ingredient, relying on your individual preferences to balance the component parts. You are also the best judge of required servings and the appetite size of yourself and your traveling companions. So all you really need is a starting point, some suggestion of what might taste good with what and basic instructions for packaging and preparing your one-liner.

At the end of this chapter you'll find a number of field-tested one-liners, many of which were adapted from recipes used at home or found on the package of one of the individual ingredients. Others were born in the process of planning meals for a 6-week ski trip, as we sat at a huge table spread with dozens of food items suited to trail use. The combinations seemed to invent themselves, and we were willing to try anything. With this approach we ended up repeating only two or three main dishes once. Everything was tasty, and nothing was boring.

After studying and perhaps trying the one-liners shared here, you'll soon be inventing your own by changing one or more of the ingredients in a line or getting a spinoff inspiration for your own concoction. New food products are to be found on the grocery store shelves each week that lend themselves well to wilderness cooking.

A POTFUL OF ONE-LINERS

Meat and Meat Substitutes

fresh precoooked meat (leftover roast, round steak; bacon; hamburger)
canned meats (boned turkey, chicken, luncheon meat, Vienna sausage)
dried chipped beef
jerky (beef or fowl, in small bits)
dried fish
smoked fish
canned fish (clams, tuna, salmon, sardines, crab, shrimp)
dry salami
Thuringer sausage
Landjager sausage
pepperoni
smoked link sausages
Canadian bacon
canned precooked bacon
bacon or meat bar
TVP (textured vegetable protein, granular and chunk form; beef, ham, chicken, bacon flavors)
nut burger mix
freeze-dried ham, beef, chicken, shrimp

Pasta, Grains, and Other Bases

spaghetti (thin)
noodles (narrow)
  egg
  whole wheat
  spinach
alphabet pasta
macaroni (small)
  egg
  whole wheat
  vegetable
rice (quick white, brown, wild)
couscous
bulgur
millet
buckwheat groats
bean threads
ramen noodles (several kinds)
chow mein noodles
freeze-dried tofu
boxed mixes such as macaroni and cheese, noodle/rice dinners
Hamburger Helper
Tuna Helper
Chicken Helper

Vegetables

fresh ones that travel well:
carrots
onions
potatoes
summer squash
cucumbers
frozen vegetables (on short trips in cool weather)
freeze-dried (many kinds)
home-dried (almost anything is possible)
commercially dried, sold in grocery stores:
onions
mushrooms
soup blends
mixed vegetable flakes
green and red pepper flakes
celery flakes
green chili peppers
potatoes: instant mashed, diced, shredded, sliced

Sauces (many available in powdered form in foil packets)	Seasonings	Toppings and Extra Additions
cheese (add dry milk)	salt, pepper	nuts (chopped, slivered)
sour-cream sauce (add dry milk)	herbs (sage, basil, oregano, etc.)	toasted sunflower seed kernels
Stroganoff (add dry milk or sour cream to most)	poultry seasoning	toasted pumpkin seeds
	paprika	coconut (shredded, flaked)
	chili powder	
spaghetti (choose one that needs only water)	dry mustard	cheese (cubed, sliced, grated)
	powdered dill	
	celery seed	margarine
powdered soup mixes (many kinds, both instant and cooked)	garlic (fresh or dried; minced, powdered)	sesame seeds
		toasted wheat germ
	garlic salt	roasted soybeans
	onion salt	bacon bits
miso powder	onion powder	croutons
gravy mix (many kinds)	celery salt	dumplings
	dried parsley flakes	instant dry milk
curry		dried pineapple bits
sweet and sour (choose one that needs only water)	dried chives	
	Butter Buds	dried or fresh diced apple
	margarine	
	powdered tomato juice	other dried fruit bits
au jus		
teriyaki	Worcestershire sauce	dried seaweed
tomato leather (page 151)	soy sauce	catsup (individual packets)
	bouillon (cubes or powder; beef, fish, chicken, vegetable)	
thickeners:		
cornstarch		
flour	mixes:	
cornmeal	chili	
	taco	
	sloppy joe	
	salad dressing	

Instructions

To create a one-liner (meal-in-a-pot), select one item from each column and combine them in the quantities you estimate you need. Use your imagination and your taste buds to determine what items will taste good together. Some proven, savory combinations are listed below. General instructions for planning and preparing one-liners are on pages 90–92.

A SAMPLING OF ONE-LINERS

Quick rice · canned chicken or chicken TVP · cream of chicken soup mix · dried onion flakes · Monterey Jack cheese

Quick rice · freeze-dried or dehydrated peas · freeze-dried ham · cheese sauce

Quick rice · sweet-and-sour sauce mix · canned chicken or ham · dried pineapple bits · cashews

Quick rice · tuna · freeze-dried peas · curry sauce mix · flaked coconut

Quick rice · dried chopped apricots, dates and raisins · curry powder · roasted peanuts

Quick brown and wild rice · precooked beef chunks · dried mushrooms and onions · Stroganoff sauce mix · sour-cream sauce mix

Quick brown rice · dried fish · sliced fresh or dried zucchini · teriyaki sauce mix

Quick brown rice · bacon bar or precooked bacon · dried tomato slices, pepper and onion flakes · white sauce mix

Quick brown rice · canned or dried shrimp · freeze-dried green beans · teriyaki sauce mix

Fried-rice mix · bacon bits · sliced green onions

Chicken-flavored Rice-a-Roni · canned chicken · sour-cream sauce mix

Couscous · precooked hamburger seasoned with sloppy joe mix · grated Swiss cheese

Bulgur · freeze-dried corn and dried sliced mushrooms · Stroganoff sauce mix

Bulgur · leftover round steak · fresh onion · beef bouillon

Bulgur · chicken TVP · dried onion and garlic · chicken bouillon · curry powder

Bulgur and soy grits · sliced fresh carrots and onions · onion soup mix · cashews

Whole wheat spaghetti · granular beef TVP · dried onion · spaghetti sauce mix · Parmesan cheese

Spinach noodles · sliced sausage · sour-cream sauce mix · Romano cheese

Egg noodles · chipped beef · dried tomato slices · tomato soup mix · mushroom soup mix

Egg noodles · canned luncheon meat · cream-of-chicken-soup mix · cream cheese · paprika, marjoram, pepper, margarine

Alphabet pasta · freeze-dried corn · turkey jerky bits · slivered almonds

Mixed-vegetable noodles · Vienna sausage · dried celery and pepper flakes · tomato soup mix

Whole wheat noodles · tuna · onion soup
mix · toasted sunflower seed kernels

Ramen noodles · beef jerky bits · dried
tomatoes · onion and pepper flakes

Brown rice ramen · sliced carrots · cream-of-
vegetable-soup mix · sesame seeds

Macaroni and cheese · tuna

Vegetable macaroni · salami chunks · cream-of-
mushroom-soup mix · cubed Cheddar cheese

Macaroni and cheese · canned salmon · dried parsley
flakes

Whole wheat macaroni · dried mushrooms, carrots
and split-pea grits · garlic powder · grated Parmesan
cheese

Instant potato flakes · crumbled meat bar · dried
mixed vegetables · gravy mix

Dried shredded potatoes · precooked beef
chunks · gravy mix

Dried potato slices · precooked bacon · freeze-dried
green beans · cheese sauce mix

Bean threads · canned chicken · powdered
miso · thin-sliced celery

HOW TO LABEL THE BAG
CONTAINING YOUR ONE-LINER

Tell what it is and how to prepare it in as few words as possible.
These instructions should be so clear and simple that any person
in your group can be the cook. (What if you're laid up in the

tent with the blahs?) Pack the main ingredients in a bread bag, produce bag, or ziplock bag; use smaller bags for separate toppings and such.

1. *Determine the order of preparation* so that you'll know what can be dumped together in one large bag and what needs to be packaged separately and then tossed into the large bag.

For example: You are putting together a rice/TVP/vegetable/sour cream sauce/soup dish. Directions with the rice say to simmer it for 8 minutes. The TVP needs about 8 minutes in water. Directions with freeze-dried vegetables say to cover them with boiling water for 10 minutes. The sour-cream sauce mix needs to sit for a few minutes to thicken and then be added last.

So . . . since the rice can "simmer" and the vegetables be "covered with boiling water" all in one operation, these two (along with salt) go into one bag. The TVP can also go in this bag, since it needs about that amount of time in water.

Into a small ziplock bag go the sour-cream sauce mix, dry soup powder and instant dry milk needed for the sauce. In camp you'll add the right amount of water to this bag, seal and mix, then let sit until the sauce has thickened.

The sour cream bag tucks into the larger one, and the whole thing gets closed and labeled. Thus, with one grab you can find all the ingredients for the entire dish.

2. *Decide how much water* to start with.

For example: If separately the ingredients call for 2 cups water for the rice, 1 cup for the vegetables and 1 cup for the TVP, compromise at $3\frac{1}{2}$ cups to start with, adding more toward the end if the mixture is too thick or dry. (It's easier to fix if you have too little water than if you have too much.)

3. *Study the instructions for each component* in order to be sure you include margarine, seasonings, instant dry milk or other items called for on the package.

4. *Determine the cooking time required* and arrive at a reasonable compromise for the combined ingredients. You'll find yourself settling for less exactness in your wilderness cooking and will discover happily that the end results taste dandy anyway!

For example: If rice simmers for 8 minutes and freeze-dried peas soak in boiling water for 10 minutes, simmer both together for 9 minutes.

5. *Summarize* all this information about ingredients, cooking time, order of preparation and so on into simple, concise instructions for each package.

For example: On the sour cream and soup bag, you might write "sauce + 1 c. water." On the larger bag which contains everything, you might write "rice/beef/vegs—simmer 9 mins. in 3½ c. water, + sauce, cook 1 min."

You'll find that with a little practice you can condense the printed instructions given on packages from several packages down to several words. I sometimes think the lengthy instructions are there to justify all the packaging.

6. *Make labels:* Write your shorthand instructions on strips of freezer tape using an indelible felt-tipped pen, and stick onto the bags. Use abbreviations wherever possible, but don't be so cryptic that an interpreter is needed if you're not the cook. You don't want to be indispensable in the backcountry kitchen, or you'll end up doing all the cooking.

GENERAL RULES FOR PACKAGING AND COOKING ONE-LINERS

- Package pasta or grains and bouillon together, along with salt for the cooking water.
- Add dried vegetables at the start of the cooking process to assure adequate rehydration. If you are using very large or hard pieces of vegetables, you may want to presoak these some before you begin cooking.
- Rice: If you would steam it at home, simmer gently in camp.
- For a pasta/sauce dish, package the pasta separately. It needs to tumble freely in boiling water in order to get tender, so you'll add sauce mix later.

- If a dish is served with a topping (such as slivered nuts, coconut, Parmesan cheese, bacon bits or sunflower seed kernels), package this in a separate bag.
- If cheese is called for, either bag it with the rest of the ingredients OR write " + cheese" on the label and re-member to slice some into the pot from the larger piece of cheese in the general food bag.
- Most one-liners are enhanced in both flavor and nutrition by the addition of a generous dab of margarine.

In camp, the usual cooking procedure is:

1. Start cooking carbohydrate base, vegetables and meat substitute.
2. Add sauce mix, cook until thick. If using canned or precooked meat, add it now, just to heat through.
3. Add topping if called for, and serve.

Sometimes when you're planning foods for a trip, one particular requirement—whether fast, light or cheap—has a high priority. One-liners take readily to adaptations in those directions. There's almost always a way to fiddle with a basic combination of ingredients and make it suit your needs, while the resulting taste and nutrition remain true to the original.

Here's a summary of suggestions you might find useful. Some variations accomplish two (even three) ends at once!

QUICK

- Thin-sliced fresh veggies instead of freeze-dried or dehydrated
- Instant potatoes instead of fresh
- Presoaked veggies to cut cooking time
- Almost instant rehydration: dehydrated sliced tomatoes and mushrooms
- Salami chunks
- Canned meat or fish

- Meat bar (outdoor store)
- Instant soup powder or gravy mix for sauce
- Ramen noodles . . . quickest of the pastas!
- Alphabet pasta
- Skinny noodles, small macaroni
- Egg pasta instead of whole wheat
- Couscous . . . almost-instant grain

LIGHT

- Short cooking times to save heavy fuel
- Instant potatoes instead of fresh
- Instant potatoes instead of rice
- TVP instead of canned turkey or chicken or beef
- Freeze-dried meats and vegetables
- Dehydrated meats, fish, vegetables
- Small bits of jerky in a main dish
- Tomato leather made from sauce or paste (page 151)
- Noodle dinners (grocery store, minus box)
- Couscous
- Bean threads
- Ramen noodles
- Freeze-dried tofu
- Butter Buds instead of margarine
- Powdered cheese spread
- Dried seaweed
- Miso powder

CHEAP

- TVP instead of any other meat form
- Cooked meat from home instead of freeze-dried or canned
- Home-dehydrated jerky, vegetables, fruit
- Fresh vegetables instead of freeze-dried
- Bulgur (especially bought in bulk)
- Pastas and grains bought in bulk or large packages
- Spices (bought in bulk) for a gourmet touch
- Extra protein: nuts, sunflower seed kernels, instant dry milk
- "Store-bought" main dishes concocted on your own from ingredients listed on package

11

~~~

Just Desserts

*F*inish your evening meal with simplicity—a couple of dried
dates, some hard candies—or elegance—a warm fruit cobbler. Choose from a limitless variety of items and ways to go,
according to how much time, effort, money and ingenuity you
want to invest.

Remember to plan ahead when cold water is needed for mixing instant puddings and such: After filling your bottle with treated
water, anchor it securely in a stream or lake for 15 minutes or
more.

NO-COOK DESSERTS

They take less time, need no pots or cleanup.

- Dried fruits, perhaps fancied up with a spread of peanut
  butter or cream cheese and chopped nuts.

- Fruit Stacks: Include in your food supply a package of condensed mincemeat. Shave thin slices to top dried peach or pear halves. Save some of the mincemeat to crumble into vanilla or lemon pudding the next night.
- Sturdy cookies: fig bars, your own brownies, date or oatmeal bars.
- Rice Krispie Marshmallow Squares: bulky but light-weight and scrumptious; they travel well.
- Instant pudding, carried and mixed in a ziplock bag. (Don't forget the dry milk!) Added touches: coconut, chocolate, carob or butterscotch chips, malted milk powder, cookie crumbs, granola, trail mix.
- Freeze-dried offerings such as gelatin, single or com-bined fruits and strawberry, chocolate or vanilla ice cream (eaten dry, with a texture like the inside of malted milk balls—expensive but fun).

FROM THE GROCERY STORE SHELVES

Using economical and tasty grocery store items, you can dupli-cate many of the more expensive dessert choices from the out-door store.

Cheesecake

Both Jell-O and Royal put out a very adequate packaged mix that sometimes includes a small packet of cherry or strawberry topping. *At home:* repackage the filling mix with the instant dry milk in a 1-quart ziplock bag. Prepare crumb crust (combine crumbs, sugar and melted margarine in a bowl), then put in a separate bag. *In camp:* add appropriate amount of water to filling mix, seal bag, and knead to mix. Pour filling into each person's bowl and sprinkle the crumb mixture on top.

Traveling Grasshopper Pie
(SERVES 3 OR 4)

At home, pack together in a 1-quart ziplock bag:

1 small package instant pistachio pudding

²/₃ cup instant dry milk

¹/₂ teaspoon mint flavoring (or, for real pizzazz, pack crème de menthe in a film cannister)

Smash and bag separately: 12 chocolate-filled chocolate sandwich cookies.
In camp: Add 1³/₄ cups cold water to the pudding bag, seal and knead to mix thoroughly. Chill a few minutes to thicken if possible. Into each bowl put a layer of cookie crumbs, pudding, more crumbs.

Four-Minute Fudge

Use a mix for a rich, rich treat. The powder is heated for a few minutes with water and margarine; add chopped nuts and set aside to firm up (in a snowbank if possible) while you eat the main course.

Raspberry or Strawberry Danish Dessert

This mix requires a few minutes cooking and stirring. It is tart and delicious either warm or cold.

Quick Rice Desserts

Quick rice is easy to dress up. As you add it to the hot water, toss in one of these:

raisins
dried banana chips
dried pineapple and apricot bits

bite-sized pieces of fruit leather
chunks of unpared fresh apple

Or, after the rice is cooked, stir in your choice of:

ground cinnamon and nutmeg
chopped nuts
sweetened coconut shreds or
  flakes

fresh berries
jam

Combine cooked rice with any flavor of prepared instant pudding, or with stewed fruits.

Baked Desserts

Mixes from the grocery store can provide an abundant variety of baked desserts (see "Bake Up a Storm!" pages 122–126).

FRUIT DESSERTS

Stewed Fruit Compote

At home, bag dried fruits (about ½ cup per serving), sugar and a little spice if you like (ground cinnamon, nutmeg, cloves). Chopped nuts are another tasty addition. *In camp:* Cooking time can be cut by presoaking fruit in water to cover, but if fruit is in fairly small pieces, this isn't needed. Cook in water to cover until tender, usually 8 to 12 minutes.

Make a double batch: half can be eaten hot with dinner and the other half saved for breakfast. Some delicious combinations are:

- pear/apricot
- cranberry (yes, dried!)/apple or pear
- cherry/apple
- huckleberry (fresh or dried)/pear
- and on ... and on ...

One step more and you have an elegant ...

Fruit Cobbler

At home: Package dried fruit as above. Add a prepacked dough mix (blend and pack in a 1-quart ziplock bag: 2 cups biscuit mix, ⅓ cup instant dry milk, ⅓ cup brown sugar, spices to taste, ¼ cup margarine). *In camp:* Add enough water to make a fairly stiff dough, seal the bag and knead with your fingers. When the fruit is not quite tender, squeeze this dough evenly over it, push it down into the hot fruit a little, cover lightly and cook for 8 minutes longer. The cobbler topping should be dry inside.

Next trip, vary this dessert by using cake mix (white, yellow or spicy) or gingerbread mix as the cobbler topping.

Apple–Peach Crunch

(SERVES 4)

At home, bag together:

2 cups mixed dried apple and peach slices	1 to 2 teaspoons date sugar (optional)
½ teaspoon ground cinnamon	

Blend and pack in a 1-quart ziplock bag:

¼ cup whole wheat flour	¼ teaspoon ground cloves
¼ cup brown sugar	1 tablespoon margarine
½ teaspoon ground cinnamon	½ cup chopped walnuts

In camp: Cook fruits in water to cover until they begin to soften. Add 1 to 2 tablespoons water to topping mix in bag, seal and knead to blend. Sprinkle on hot fruit and cook, uncovered, for 5 minutes.

AND TWO DELECTABLE HOME-MADE PUDDINGS

Fruited Pudding

(4 LARGE SERVINGS)

At home, bag together:

1½ cups chopped dried apples
1½ cups chopped dried apricots
¼ cup brown sugar

½ teaspoon ground cinnamon
½ teaspoon ground nutmeg

In another bag, pack:

2 tablespoons quick-cooking tapioca

½ cup instant dry milk

Bag separately: ¾ cup chopped walnuts.

In camp: Simmer fruits in 5 cups water for 6 minutes. Turn the stove down a bit and gradually blend in dry milk and tapioca, stirring to dissolve thoroughly. Simmer and stir for 2 to 3 minutes; add nuts and serve.

Fast and Creamy Pudding

cooks in just a few minutes and tastes much better than instant mixes. This amount of mix makes two batches of 4 servings each. Stir together until very well blended:

1¾ cups instant dry milk
½ cup cornstarch

¾ cup sugar
½ teaspoon salt

Divide in half and add flavorings from the following list as desired. Carry in ziplock bags:

coconut: add 2 tablespoons sweetened coconut flakes to mix, plus ¼ teaspoon ground nutmeg

carob: add ¼ cup sifted carob powder to mix, plus ½ teaspoon ground cinnamon

other: add ½ cup candy bits or ½ cup chopped nuts

In camp: Blend ½ cup water into mix in bag, seal and knead to a well-blended paste. Heat 1¾ cups water to boiling. Gradually stir paste into water, stirring constantly until it simmers and thickens (about 2 minutes). Serve warm.

12

~~~~~

Snacks to Make at Home

A ll these foods freeze well; some keep for weeks in a cool, dry place. Package in trail-use portions, seal well and label. When trip-planning time is short, having these on hand means you can eat as if you had planned for days!

Gorp

(THE FAMOUS TRAIL SNACK)

Any eclectic combination of nuts, seeds, dried fruits, candies and such. To help meet your body's needs, use *salted* nuts and avoid the *dry* roasted ones, since you need fats. Some favorite gorp blends:

- raisins/almonds
- chopped dates/chopped walnuts/shredded coconut
- dried papaya/dried pineapple/licorice candies/peanuts

- butterscotch bits/walnut halves/raisins
- roasted cashews/M & M's/raisins
- roasted pumpkin seeds/dried apple bits/toasted coconut flakes
- mixed salted nuts/dried banana chips/chopped dates
- chocolate bits/toasted sunflower seed kernels/salted peanuts/dried banana chips

The following two gorpish candies are made into big, rich squares. If the weather is very hot, you may find these nuggets have melted into other interesting shapes (unless you bury them deep in your pack). These substantial snacks are also great desserts.

Mountain Bars

12 ounces butterscotch chips   ½ cup chopped nuts
½ cup honey

½ cup each:

toasted wheat germ   coconut (flaked
raisins   or shredded)

Melt chips in a double boiler; blend in honey. Add all remaining ingredients, stirring quickly to blend well. Pat mixture into a greased 9-inch square pan. When partly cool, cut into 36 1½-inch squares. Store in refrigerator or freezer.

Gorp Squares

12 ounces chocolate chips   1 cup uncooked quick oatmeal
6 ounces butterscotch chips

½ cup each:

honey   broken cashews
chopped dates   walnuts
OR prunes   OR almonds
golden raisins   OR peanuts
shredded coconut   toasted wheat germ

Melt chips in a double boiler; blend in honey. Pour over remaining ingredients in a large bowl. Mix well; pour into a greased 9-by-14-inch pan. When partly cool, cut into squares. Store in refrigerator or freezer.

Fruit Balls

Grind together dried figs and raisins; mix in some peanut butter and flaked coconut. Shape into balls; roll in chopped nuts or sesame seeds.

Spicy Seeds

Toast pumpkin seeds and sunflower seed kernels in margarine over low heat until the pumpkin seeds are slightly puffy. Season with salt, soy sauce, chili powder; stir well.

TRAILPROOF COOKIES

Peanut Butter Supercookies

(MAKES 18 *HUGE ONES*)

Preheat oven to 350°F. Cream together:

1 cup margarine

1 cup chunky peanut butter

Add:

1¾ cups brown sugar
2 eggs, beaten

¼ teaspoon vanilla extract

Mix in:

2 cups whole wheat flour

2 teaspoons baking powder

Add:

2 cups granola OR quick oatmeal OR 1 cup raisins and 1
   cup chopped roasted peanuts

Drop by huge spoonfuls onto a greased cookie sheet and flatten with a fork. Bake for 10 to 12 minutes.

Trekker Treats

(MAKES 12 BARS)

Preheat oven to 350° F.
Blend in a large bowl:

¾ cup whole wheat flour	¼ cup toasted wheat germ
½ cup quick oatmeal	½ cup brown sugar
½ cup softened margarine	grated peel of 1 orange

Pat this mixture into an oiled 9-inch square pan. In a small bowl, beat 2 eggs with ¼ cup brown sugar, then stir in ¼ cup *each* chopped walnuts, slivered almonds and shredded coconut. Pour this mixture over the patted-down mixture and bake for 30 minutes. Let cool completely, then cut into 12 bars. Wrap individually in foil or plastic wrap.

Honey–Nut Bars

(MAKES 12 DENSE AND CHEWY BARS, WITH LOTS OF FOOD VALUE)

Preheat oven to 350° F.
Beat together:

1 egg	1 teaspoon vanilla extract
½ cup honey	

Combine:

¾ cup whole wheat flour	½ teaspoon ground coriander
¼ cup instant dry milk	¼ teaspoon ground nutmeg
1 teaspoon baking powder	¼ teaspoon salt

Add dry ingredients to egg-honey mixture and blend well. Then add:

1 cup chopped roasted peanuts or almonds	¾ cup ground sesame seeds

Mix gently; spread batter in a greased 9-inch square pan and bake for 25 to 30 minutes. Let cool and cut into 12 bars.

Butterscotch Brownies

(MAKES 12 BARS)

½ cup shortening
2 cups brown sugar
2 eggs
1½ cups sifted unbleached
   white flour

2 teaspoons baking powder
½ teaspoon salt
1 teaspoon vanilla extract
1 cup chopped walnuts

Preheat oven to 350°F. Melt shortening. Blend in brown sugar, then eggs. Sift dry ingredients together and add to first mixture. Add vanilla and nuts. Spread in an oiled and floured 9-inch square pan and bake for 25 to 35 minutes.

"SURVIVAL" RATIONS

Logan Bread

This makes a *huge* batch of sixty 2-inch squares, high in protein, vitamins, iron and calcium. Keeps weeks on the trail, longer in the refrigerator, indefinitely in the freezer.

4 pounds (14⅓ cups) whole
   wheat flour
1½ cups brown sugar
½ cup instant dry milk
1 teaspoon salt
2 teaspoons baking powder
1 teaspoon ground cinnamon
1 teaspoon ground nutmeg

1 cup chopped nuts
4 cups water
1¼ cups honey
1½ cups blackstrap molasses
   (much better nutritionally
   than regular molasses)
1¼ cups melted shortening
2 cups chopped dried fruit

Preheat oven to 300° F. To blended dry ingredients add water, then honey, molasses, shortening and fruit. Pour batter about an inch thick into greased pans and bake for 1 hour. Reduce oven to 200° F, leave door open slightly and continue to dry the bread for several hours. The drier it is, the longer it will keep.

Pemmican

A modern version of the old buffalo meat and service berry concoction. Makes 12 to 16 squares.
Preheat oven to 325°F.

Chop fine: ½ cup each:

raisins
dried apricots
dates

dried beef (Armour's thin-
    sliced, in a jar)

Add:

grated peel of 1 orange
¾ cup brown sugar
½ cup whole wheat flour
1 tablespoon each:
    vinegar
    vegetable oil
    maple syrup

1 teaspoon vanilla extract
½ egg, beaten
pinch of salt
1 teaspoon each:
    ground cinnamon
    ground nutmeg
    ground allspice

Add enough cider, brandy or rum to make a heavy dough. Blend well, then pat mixture into an oiled 9-inch square pan. Bake for at least 1 hour, until it is firm and not sticky. Let cool, then cut into 12 or 16 bars.

13

~~~~~

Fill Your Cup

An array of good and tempting drinks is important for your wilderness wanderings in several ways. It will encourage you to drink enough liquid (that 3 to 4 quarts you need each day is a lot of cups!). And snowmelt, boiled or chemically treated water is more palatable when turned into a tasty drink. Especially when they contain milk, beverages can contribute substantial nutrition. And, of course, there's nothing more spirit-lifting than a quick cooling or warming of the inner man when he needs it!

Head out on your hike with chilled water. Carrying a slice of fresh lemon in your water bottle will perk up plain water and disguise the plastic taste.

The simplest drinks are brewed from ready-made powders or cubes. Start dinner with a cup of bouillon . . . available in beef, chicken and vegetable flavors at the grocery and natural foods store.

Gourmet and imported foods sections often yield bouillon cubes in interesting fruit and herbal flavors; these drink bases usually contain a substantial amount of vitamin C and not much sugar: chamomile, rose hip, fruit blends. Hot fruit gelatin is a real body warmer on chilly mountain mornings and an easy capper to dinner. At nippy temperatures *any* fruit drink (including lemonade) tastes great hot.

Two weight-saving innovations are especially helpful to thirsty backpackers. Dehydrated honey, available in natural foods stores, is a great sweetener for tea and handy for dry beverage mixes, since it is soluble in either cold or hot water. Fruit drink powders are now available sweetened with Nutrasweet instead of heavy, bulky sugar. (Just 1 teaspoon makes a *quart* of drink!)

BEVERAGE BLENDS

Keep jars of these mixes on your pantry shelves, ready to be tapped for trips.

Rich Trail Cocoa

A *big* batch! You may want to divide it in half and turn part into Mexican Chocolate with the addition of 1 to 2 teaspoons ground cinnamon.

At home, mix together:

1-pound instant cocoa mix	8 quarts (11 cups) instant dry
6 ounces nondairy creamer	milk
	⅔ cup brown sugar

In camp: Use ⅓ cup mix in 1 cup *hot* water.

Russian Tea

Spicy and fragrant.
At home, mix together:

1 cup powdered orange break-	1-quart lemonade mix packet
fast drink	½ to 1 teaspoon each: ground
½ cup sugar	cinnamon, ground cloves
½ cup instant tea powder	

In camp: Use 2 to 4 tablespoons mix in 1 cup *hot* water.

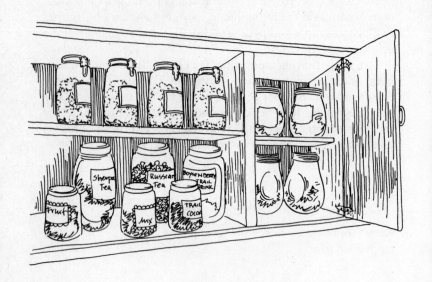

Sherpa Tea

A rich pick-me-up, especially in crisp weather.
At home, mix together:

2 cups instant dry milk
⅓ cup sugar

2 tablespoons instant tea powder

In camp: Use 2 to 3 tablespoons mix with a dab of margarine in a cup of *hot* water.

Mexican Mocha

Ole!
At home, mix together:

1½ cups instant cocoa mix
1½ cups instant dry milk
½ cup instant coffee powder

1 teaspoon ground cinnamon
1 tablespoon powdered, dried orange peel

In camp: Use ⅓ cup mix in 1 cup *hot* water.

Spiced Hot Milk

Some prefer their milk straight, but dry milk mixed with cold water isn't all that tasty. Here's a more palatable version.
At home, mix together:

2 cups instant dry milk
1 tablespoon ground cinnamon
½ teaspoon ground nutmeg

¼ cup brown sugar OR dehydrated honey

In camp: Put ⅓ cup mix in your cup, then slowly fill with *hot* water as you stir.

Creamy Orange Cooler

Remember the Creamsicles you loved as a kid? This drink will take you back.
At home, mix together:

2 cups instant dry milk

1¼ cups powdered orange
breakfast drink

In camp: Blend ⅓ cup mix with each cup *cold* water.

Hot Malt

A hefty addition to the day's protein quota, good with breakfast or dinner.
At home, mix together:

2 cups instant dry milk

½ cup malted milk powder

In camp: Put ⅓ cup mix in your cup, then slowly fill with *hot* water as you stir.

Carob–Malt Smoothie

Rich and sweet.
At home, mix together:

2 cups instant dry milk	½ cup sifted carob powder
½ cup malted milk powder	¼ cup brown sugar

In camp: Put ⅓ cup mix in your cup, then slowly fill with *hot* water as you stir.

Eggnog Drink

Richer, but less expensive than the individual packets you can buy.
At home, mix together:

1½ cups instant dry milk	2 tablespoons brown sugar
½ cup nondairy creamer	½ teaspoon ground cinnamon
½ cup powdered egg mix	½ teaspoon ground nutmeg

In camp: Put ⅓ cup mix in your cup and stir in *cold* water to fill. Sprinkle with additional nutmeg.

Trail Shakes

These were handier in the days before hikers needed to treat most water to make it safe. But with a little forethought you can still enjoy their creamy richness. Boiled water can be quickly cooled by anchoring your bottle in a lake or stream, and most chemical treatments simply need to sit in cold water 30 minutes or so. Filtered water stays cold, of course.
At home, mix together:

2 cups instant dry milk	2 tablespoons whole wheat flour
½ cup nondairy creamer	3 tablespoons brown sugar

To this basic mix, add ½ cup of your choice of the following flavorings:

- instant cocoa mix (the kind that will dissolve in *cold* water)

- instant coffee powder
- finely ground nuts
- crushed dried banana chips
- finely flaked coconut
- powdered berry syrup mix

Or, *in camp,* add a hefty blob of jam for each serving. Pack ½ cup mix in a ziplock bag for each 1-cup serving.

In camp: Add ¾ cup *cold* water per serving, seal and shake the bag vigorously until all the dry ingredients are dissolved, OR combine cold water and dry mix in your water bottle, screw the lid on tightly, shake vigorously.

Also see these beverage recipes:
Instant Breakfast Drinks
(page 129)
Flavored Coffee Mixes
(pages 129–130)

14

~~~~~~

Gourmet Feasting

Sometimes when backpacking, a truly elegant meal is in order...perhaps to celebrate a reunion of old friends, a mountain climb, a birthday or anniversary. Terrific food is one essential ingredient, of course, but first dip into your pack for the makings of a special "table" setting.

SET A CLASSY TABLE

A bright poncho, small tarp or space blanket can double as a tablecloth, and print bandanas make fine napkins. When planning a celebrative spread, I pack wooden bowls and spoons (chopsticks for a stir fry) and small plastic wineglasses. The squat, scented votive candle in my emergency kit becomes the focus for a centerpiece that incorporates bits of natural beauty such as leaves and cones. I know one gourmet chef with flair: He dresses for dinner in a T-shirt printed like a tuxedo front!

JAZZ UP THE ORDINARY

There are countless easy and inexpensive ways to add pizzazz to commonplace trail foods, so you needn't spend a bundle on exotic foods unless you want to. Often just one elegant touch will make a meal memorable.

Carry herb and spice blends or a smidgen of sherry or soy sauce in plastic film cannisters. Prowl the gourmet section of your grocery store for foil-packed sauce mixes to serve atop rice, pasta, cooked vegetables or English muffins. You'll find béarnaise, sweet and sour, curry, honey–mustard, hunter's, Cheddar cheese, teriyaki and others. Even ordinary noodles turn gourmet when topped with herby pesto sauce (a dry mix is sold in natural foods stores).

The unexpected also livens up meals: cashews, almonds or peanuts add crunch and flavor to a main dish; a sprinkling of pine nuts or sesame seeds on vegetables is a surprise; dried seaweed crumbled atop a freeze-dried entree or dried oriental mushrooms cooked with it lift it from the ordinary; combinations such as tomato–pea soup are different and delicious.

Introduce variety by serving different pastas or grains (again, search the natural foods store, outdoor store or the grocery store's gourmet aisle): pilaf, wild rice, bulgur, buckwheat groats, vegetable pastas in many shapes and colors, quick brown rice, couscous, millet, bean threads, vermicelli and rice blends.

GREAT BEGINNINGS

Preface an otherwise ho-hum dinner with some unusual soup: asparagus, oxtail, leek, fish chowder, minestrone with Parmesan cheese topping, spiced tomato with a cinnamon stick stirrer. Or open with fresh melon balls and stemmed grapes. Packed at home in a plastic bag or carton, they'll keep several days and provide a welcome change from dried fare. Kiwi fruits also travel well, and their bright green juiciness is elegant and delicious.

Workaday raw veggies or crackers take on a whole new character when dunked in a zippy dip, and there are endless possibilities. Try:

- Powdered guacamole dip mix (grocery store) to blend with avocados (packed firm, they'll soften in 2 or 3 days)
- Powdered hummus (spiced Middle Eastern garbanzo bean dip, found in natural foods store or gourmet section)
- Cream cheese blended at home with horseradish and chopped smoked meats

Herbed Appetizer Dip

(FOR 2)

At home: Empty a packet of sour-cream sauce mix into a 1-quart ziplock bag along with ¼ cup instant dry milk, a bit of dried chives, dashes of ground pepper and garlic salt and ¼ teaspoon dried tarragon. *In camp:* Add ½ cup cold water to the bag, seal and mix well by kneading with your fingers. Set aside a few minutes to thicken. Leftovers are unlikely, but they can be added to your next soup or plainish one-pot dish.

Merely venturing beyond carrot and celery sticks lends a fresh touch; dip crisp raw green beans, cauliflower, broccoli, jicama, turnips, cucumber, green pepper, summer squash, sunchokes. Crackers, too, can be had in dozens of shapes and flavors.

Slices of salami (get a "dry" kind that needs no refrigeration) dunk admirably well in all of the above mixtures, but the *supreme* spread for salami came my way on a recent mountain journey. It keeps for weeks in the refrigerator, so make this big batch and carry what you need for a trip in a film cannister or other small leakproof container.

Happy's Hot Mustard

(MAKES 3 CUPS)

½ cup plus 1 tablespoon dry mustard
1½ cups sifted white flour
1 cup sugar
½ teaspoon salt

1 egg
1 cup white vinegar
1½ teaspoons melted margarine

Blend dry ingredients and add egg. Then add vinegar slowly while beating with a mixer. Stir in melted margarine. Store in refrigerator.

My hot-mustard friend travels with real class. On one hike she produced a chilled foil-wrapped bundle from the deep recesses of her pack (where it had been snuggling next to plastic vanilla bottles full of ice made at home by filling bottles with water and putting them in the freezer), then served up this ambrosial appetizer:

Ham–Pineapple Rollups

Spread thin slices of ham with cream cheese mixed with pineapple. Roll or fold into tidy bundles and chill well before packing.

Entrees to Remember

Highlight your festive board with one of these rich, unusual main dishes.

Swimmer in the Garden

(SERVES 2)

If you're lucky (or is it skilled?) enough to have fresh trout, it can be the basis for this fine and fancy main dish. It uses some fresh veggies that travel well, an unusual and very quick-cooking grain and a nice touch of herbs. In high country you may find tart alpine sorrel leaves tucked among the rocks. This lemony green makes a refreshing and colorful garnish for fish dishes.

1 medium onion
4 carrots
1 medium zucchini
1 medium or 2 small trout

coating mix packed in a large plastic bag:
¾ cup cornmeal
1 teaspoon dried dillweed
½ teaspoon salt
pepper
¾ cup couscous
¼ cup margarine

Cut veggies into bite-sized chunks. Clean fish, dampen and shake in coating bag. Pour 1½ cups boiling water onto couscous in a small pan; cover and set aside, wrapped in a pad or coat to stay warm.

Melt margarine in a frying pan, then stir fry veggies for a few minutes. Push to the side, add fish and cook for about 5 minutes. When browned, turn fish to cook on its other side, stirring the veggies occasionally. When fish flakes easily, it's done.

Fluff the couscous and place a bed of it in each bowl, then top with veggies and fish. Pour the wine, toast the occasion and enjoy!

Eagle Cap Rice and Riches

(4 HEARTY SERVINGS)

At home, pack:

1 medium fresh onion
2 tablespoons margarine
2 cups quick rice

1 package Knorr's Oxtail Soup
Mix
1 cup salami chunks

In camp: Peel and chop onion; sauté in margarine until transparent, then add rice and 5 cups hot water. Partially cover and cook until rice is almost tender. Blend in soup mix, adding more water if too thick. Cook for 5 minutes, then add chunked salami and heat through.

Oriental Treasure Pot

(2 HEARTY OR 3 MEDIUM SERVINGS)

1 package (3.1 oz.) freeze-dried
tofu (natural foods store)
1 package (3.1 oz.) 5-spice
ramen (natural foods store or
outdoor store)

1½ cups fresh or frozen snow
peas (pea pods)

Prepare freeze-dried tofu with hot water according to directions on the box. Keep warm while you cook the ramen and peas together in 2 cups boiling water. When almost tender, blend in the spice packet, and chunked tofu if using fresh. Or put reconstituted freeze-dried tofu into each person's bowl, then top with the spiced ramen and peas.

Creamed Turkey with a Difference

(SERVES 4)

At home, package together:

12 to 16 ounces thin spaghetti
2 cubes chicken bouillon

1 teaspoon dried chopped
onion

Into a 1-quart ziplock bag, empty a foil packet of sour-cream sauce mix and ⅓ cup instant dry milk. Also pack:

two 5-ounce cans boned turkey
2 single-serving envelopes
  cream-of-vegetable-soup mix
½ cup slivered almonds

1 double-serving package of
  freeze-dried peas OR one 10-
  ounce package frozen peas
  (wrapped to stay cold)

In camp: Mix ½ cup cold water into the sour cream bag and set aside. To 5 cups boiling water, add the pasta, seasonings and peas. Simmer for 5 minutes; add chunked turkey, then stir in soup powder. Add more water if needed. Serve with a sprinkling of almonds on each portion.

Mulligatawny

(4 HEARTY SERVINGS)

At home, pack:

2 cups quick rice
one 4-serving package Mulliga-
  tawny Soup Mix (gourmet
  shelf or natural foods store)
¼ cup instant dry milk

1 tablespoon margarine
dry sherry in a film cannister
  (optional)
1 unpared red apple

In camp: Prepare rice according to directions and keep warm while making the sauce. Blend soup mix and dry milk into 2 cups cold water in pan. Add margarine and gently bring to a boil while stirring. Simmer for 2 minutes, stirring constantly. Add sherry if desired. Pour over cooked rice and top generously with small dices of unpared apple.

GRAND FINALES

Choose a dessert fillip for your feast from this collection.

The easiest elegant treats

- Bars of halvah (creamy sesame candy)
- Sweet dried pineapple rings

- Dressups for applesauce or stewed fruits:
    small snips of wild-ginger rootstock
    chopped dates
    a handful of slivered almonds
    ground cinnamon, nutmeg, allspice
    a sprinkling of toasted shredded coconut
- Fresh papaya with lime juice (for two: pack 1 ripe papaya and a lime. Halve fruit, scoop out seeds, divide lime. Each diner squeezes lime juice onto his papaya half as he eats.)

A bit more preparation
Sunshine Lake Hot Fudge Sundaes

What? On the trail?!? *At home,* pack:

Magic Shell chocolate syrup in plastic dispenser bottle
dried banana chips

freeze-dried vanilla or chocolate ice cream (2 servings per package)

In camp: Float syrup bottle in water as it heats for coffee. In each bowl, put a handful of ice cream chunks, then some banana chips. Shake the heated syrup well and squeeze on top. Forget the "wet" sundaes you've eaten, and enjoy this backwoods version. When your bowl is empty, a cup of coffee turns into mocha as the last of the fudge topping dissolves.

Sundae variations:

- Top with peanuts or walnuts
- Cap strawberry ice cream with dried sliced strawberries . . . let them melt in your mouth.
- Soften dehydrated or freeze-dried peaches, blueberries or apples in hot water to cover; when cool, pour over freeze-dried ice cream chunks, liquid and all.

Sweet and Saucy Cake

(BAKE AND PREPACKAGE AT HOME;
2 CUPS SAUCE MAKES 4 SERVINGS)

Use vanilla sauce mix from the import store or gourmet shelf to top slices of the rich breads on pages 63–65: Pumpkin, Spicy Apple, Zucchini.

At home: Prepackage the sauce mix with ⅔ cup instant dry milk and 2 tablespoons sugar.

In camp: Stir mix into 2 cups water and gently bring to a boil. Pour the warm sauce over thick slices of sweet dessert bread.

Pumpkin–Nut Pudding

(4 SMALL OR 3 MEDIUM SERVINGS)

At home, package together in a 1-quart ziplock bag:

1 small package instant vanilla pudding
⅓ cup instant dry milk

¼ teaspoon each: ground nutmeg and ground cloves

In a separate container with a tight lid, put ½ cup canned pumpkin pie filling. Also pack ½ cup chopped walnuts.

In camp: Add 1¼ cups cold water to the pudding bag, seal and mix well, then add pumpkin and blend well. Top each serving with a sprinkling of nuts.

Anne's Tipsy Fruits

(4 RICH SERVINGS)

At home, pack together:

2 cups mixed dried apricots, pears and apples
½ teaspoon ground cinnamon

1 teaspoon dried grated orange or lemon peel

In a film cannister, pack mandarin orange liqueur.

In camp: Cook fruit and spices in water to cover till barely tender. Add liqueur and serve.

Variation: Pack dried apples and pineapple bits with ¼ teaspoon ground ginger; use crème de menthe liqueur.

Orange–Mincemeat Bars

Make at home; a 28-ounce jar of mincement is enough for two recipes. Why not double it and have a batch in the freezer? Preheat oven to 350° F.
Mix well:

½ cup chopped walnuts
1¼ cups quick oatmeal
1 cup flour

1 cup firmly packed brown
   sugar
½ teaspoon salt

With a pastry blender, cut in ¾ cup margarine. Pat half this mixture into a well-buttered 9-inch square pan. Combine:

1½ cups prepared mincemeat
1 unpeeled seedless orange, cut
   in large chunks and put
   through food grinder

2 tablespoons cornstarch

Spread over the crumbs, then top with the remaining crumb mixture, patting down well. Blend 1 beaten egg yolk with 2 tablespoons water; spoon over crumb mixture. Bake for 50 minutes. Let cool in pan; cut into 9 or 12 bars.

15

Bake Up a Storm!

Spicy coffee cake, hot cheese-onion bread, toasty corn muffins...*yum!* Most backpackers would welcome such fare, but deem it totally impractical. Prebaked edibles like these rarely survive intact in a pack whose every corner is allotted to socks, rain gear, tent and a dozen other necessities. And if not a crumbled mess, they quickly grow stale.

But these baked delicacies and many others *can* be prepared in camp, using a variety of gear and methods. Baking mixes are easily put together at home and packed in resealable gallon-sized ziplock bags, which double as mixing bowls in camp.

THE METHODS

Trail baking takes about the same amount of time as it does in your oven at home, so it's for leisurely times in kindly weather.

In country where open fires are allowed and appropriate, bake your treats in a purchased ($12 and up) or homemade reflector oven set at the edge of the coals. For a workable substitute, rig a doubled-foil hood halfway around a layer cake pan.

Even the hiker who relies on a stove can turn out baked goods, choosing his method from several options. Fun, although most expensive and bulky (but you can pack your socks in it), is Optimus' Mini-Oven (about $30 ... a joint investment with friends?). Developed for use with a Svea or Optimus stove, it can also top a Coleman Peak 1 and stoves of similar design (and do a dandy job on a woodstove at home). The lidded ring pan nestles on a heat-distributing shell; heat circulates up through the center and around the batter in the pan, browning contents on all sides but the top. The best gingerbread I ever ate was baked in a friend's mini-oven in our snow camp.

Any baking mix can be cooked in the form of thick pancakes, using a frying pan on a stove. A Teflon-coated pan makes things easy, or you can pack a small leakproof container of salad oil (margarine and butter burn too readily). Don't forget to tuck in a pancake turner.

One way to stove-cook biscuits is as dumplings. Drop blobs of dough onto your bubbling main dish a few minutes before it is done, cover and steam for the remaining 8 to 10 minutes, or until the dumplings are dry inside. (Teaspoon-sized dumplings cook fastest.) This same method can produce a juicy cobbler: Cook sweetened and spiced biscuit dough atop simmering dried fruits.

THE MIXES

Whatever your cooking method, the key to this elegant yet fuss-less feasting is to do much of the preparation ahead of time, leaving simple mixing for camp.

Use instant dry milk, powdered buttermilk and powdered eggs in your home-brewed mixes; cut in margarine or shortening at home (it keeps well several days in all but the hottest weather).

If you prefer ready-made mixes, the simplest among the grocery store's abundant options are those labeled "add only water."

To use mixes that call for milk and eggs, substitute about ⅓ cup instant dry milk for each cup of liquid milk called for, and check the powdered egg package for equivalent amounts. Then

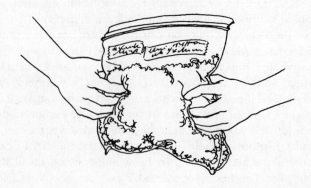

remember to include in camp instructions enough water to rehydrate these dry ingredients.

The grocery store sells mixes for biscuits, corn muffins or bread, brownies, snacking cakes and muffins of all kinds, including blueberry, date, apple, cherry and bran.

Versatile basic baking mix can be used either plain (that is, with only dry milk and margarine added at home, water in camp) or enhanced with your choice of:

chopped dried or fresh
    onion
crumbled precooked bacon
    or bacon bar
dried herbs
slivers of cheese

sunflower seed kernels
celery seeds
raisins and sugar
small snips of dried fruit
chopped nuts

Add the dried items as you prepackage the mix at home; save the fresh ones for camp. Or sometimes cook in layers: Soak dried fruits until soft in their carrying bag, then drain off (and swig down) any excess water. Put the fruits in a pan, cover with batter and bake.

A FEW CHOICE RECIPES

Here are four tasty treats—thrifty, lightweight and easily packable—to bake in camp. Two recipes make use of dried spread mixes available at outdoor stores, to add flavors that would be difficult to incorporate in their perishable form.

Peanutty Muffin Mouthfuls

Makes 20 fragrant small muffins, loaded with protein. Great with butter, jam or honey!
At home, mix together in a medium-sized bowl:

½ cup whole wheat flour
½ cup unbleached white flour
¼ cup toasted wheat germ
½ cup instant dry milk
1 double-serving packet dry
peanut butter/honey spread
mix (from the outdoor store)

1 teaspoon baking soda
2 dashes each salt and ground
cinnamon
2 tablespoons finely chopped
dried peaches, apricots or
dates (optional)

With a pastry blender, cut in 3 tablespoons margarine. Pack the mixture in a 1-gallon ziplock bag.
In camp: Add a little more than ½ cup water to the bag, seal and knead quickly until thoroughly moistened. Squeeze heaping tablespoon-sized blobs onto a greased pan and bake for about 10 to 15 minutes.

Cheddar Biscuit Gems

Makes 12 fat golden biscuits, with cheese and onion flavors that nicely accent any camp dinner. This dough can also cook as small dumplings in a covered pot of stew.
At home, blend together and pack in a 1-gallon ziplock bag:

2 cups biscuit mix
⅓ cup instant dry milk
1 double-serving packet dry
cheese spread mix (from the
outdoor store)

1 teaspoon dried chopped
onion
½ teaspoon celery seed

In camp: Add ¾ cup water, seal and knead the bag to thoroughly moisten dry ingredients. Squeeze batter onto a greased pan and bake for about 15 minutes.

Fruit Cobbler

Delicious combinations of dried fruits can form the basis of easy camp cobblers, satisfying the hankering for a juicy, sweet dessert while packing a good nutritional punch. There probably won't be any leftovers, but if there are, use them to round out tomorrow's breakfast. Start with your favorite dried fruits or try these interesting blends, using the recipe on page 97:

pears, pineapple, apricots
cherries, apples, peaches

apples, huckleberries (fresh
   or dried)
cranberries, pears

Spiced Coffee Cake

Equally good for dinner or breakfast, this adaptation of a very old recipe has sturdy flavors that are welcome companions to milder dishes.

At home, cream together in a large bowl:

½ cup sugar

2 tablespoons margarine

Then mix in:

1⅔ cups unbleached white
   flour
⅓ cup powdered buttermilk
1 teaspoon baking soda
1 teaspoon ground cinnamon

½ teaspoon ground cloves
½ teaspoon ground nutmeg
1 cup raisins

Put mix into a 1-gallon ziplock bag.

In camp: Add 1 cup water, seal and mix thoroughly by kneading the bag. Squeeze the batter into a well-greased pan and bake. If using a reflector oven, start by placing it away from the hottest part of the fire, and move it closer for browning toward the end of the baking time. Turn the pan if necessary for even cooking. Depending on the heat of your fire, this should take about 30 minutes.

16

Good Eating on a Bootlace

*B*eing a dedicated and enthusiastic conserver by nature, I've sprinkled this book with many money-saving ideas. But years of backcountry roaming and kitchen puttering have fattened my list of bargain backpack foods considerably, and I'd like to share more tips for the benefit of *your* budget. First, eight general penny-wise practices. Then, specific food suggestions.

MAXIMS FOR THE THRIFT-MINDED

- The less you pay for someone else's work or time, the cheaper foods will be.
- Commercial packaging costs, so buy in bulk, repackaging into trail quantities. *Many* common foods are available in bulk at natural foods stores and some larger grocery outlets: oatmeal, spices, nuts, granola, dried veggies, potato flakes, rice, honey, raisins, more.

- Make recipes in big quantities, freezing or otherwise storing trail portions. This saves time as well as money. Examples: beverages, main dishes, breads.
- Make your own! Examples: instant oatmeal, trail mix, granola bars, cookies, soup and sauce mixes.
- Dry your own! Especially economical if you garden, but anyone can turn out delicious and reasonably priced dried mushrooms, fruits and such, watching for sales.
- Shop at several sources instead of just one. Outdoor stores typically charge 40 percent or more above grocery store prices for items like cocoa, snack bars, fruit drinks, dried fruit, dry milk. Spices bought in bulk at the natural foods store are far cheaper than the tinned ones at the grocery store.
- Don't waste money on foods that will spoil or get smashed or on too-large quantities of a main dish. (You'll bemoan your careless planning as you pack out the garbage.)
- Use caution about things it's easy to overspend on: snacks (huge chocolate bars, hard candies, smoked nuts); protein (freeze-dried meats, canned chicken and fish); quick stuff (freeze-dried everything); convenience (individual servings, full-course meals, small packets of cheese and crackers).

INEXPENSIVE EDIBLES

Instant Oatmeal

Fixing your own costs just a fraction of the price of store-bought packets. (One of those is *never* enough for a hungry hiker, and he has to remember the milk, besides.) Make a big batch while you're at it, since the mix stores well in jars on the shelf, ready for future treks.

Start with quick oatmeal (cheapest bought in bulk) and whir a third of the amount you're using in a blender or coffee mill until powdered. This will become the thick "glue" that holds the rest together.

In a big bowl, mix: all the oatmeal, instant dry milk (⅓ cup for each cup of dry oatmeal), a touch of spice such as ground cinnamon or nutmeg, sweetening to taste (white or brown sugar, or dehydrated honey from the natural foods store).

I usually toss in a protein-enhancing handful of toasted wheat germ or wheat bran and often a bit of sesame seeds or chopped nuts for added flavor and nutrition. Bits of dried fruit (raisins, apples, banana chips, sliced strawberries, apricots and such) can be added at this point or, for more variety, when you pack each trip's portion.

Before a hike, I pack ⅓ cup of this mix per serving in a bag. In camp, I put that amount into my cup, fill it with boiling water, stir and enjoy. Cooking isn't really necessary, since a couple of minutes in hot water softens everything nicely. No messy pan!

Instant Breakfast Drinks

Your own cost about 31¢ a serving, compared with 49¢ for the commercial packets (including the milk they require).
At home, for each 1-cup serving, use this basic mix:

¼ cup instant dry milk
1 tablespoon nondairy creamer

1 tablespoon powdered egg

Add your choice of flavoring:

1 teaspoon instant coffee powder
1 tablespoon instant cocoa mix
  (for *cold* water)
for mocha, 1 tablespoon instant
  cocoa mix (for *cold* water)
  and ½ teaspoon instant coffee powder

single-serving restaurant packet
  of jam or jelly
1 tablespoon instant malted
  milk powder

In camp: Mix with *cold* water, either in your cup or seal and shake in a ziplock bag.

Flavored Coffee Mixes

Store in jars at home. Each recipe makes enough for about 16 cups of coffee. *In camp:* Use 2 teaspoons mix in each cup of hot water.

SPICED COFFEE

²/₃ cup instant coffee powder
¾ cup nondairy creamer
½ cup brown sugar OR ⅓ cup
dehydrated honey

¾ teaspoon ground cinnamon
¼ teaspoon each ground nutmeg, ground cloves, ground
allspice

ORANGE COFFEE

²/₃ cup instant coffee powder
²/₃ cup brown sugar

1 tablespoon dried and powdered orange peel
½ teaspoon ground cinnamon

WAYS TO GET PROTEIN

(WITHOUT PAYING $2 A SERVING FOR FREEZE-DRIED MEAT)

Accustomed to thinking of our major protein intake coming in
the form of breakfast eggs or dinner meat, we neglect a wealth
of other opportunities.

Protein can be added to any soup or main dish; just put in
some slivered cheese, nuts or sunflower seed kernels. Chowders
and cream soups contain more protein than clear soups. On a
long solo trip when cost, pack weight and adequate nutrition
were prime concerns, I carried a small bag of sesame meal (ground
toasted sesame seeds). Each night I stirred a big spoonful of this
almost weightless nutritional bonanza into my main dish.

Milk is an excellent and inexpensive source of protein, and
instant dry milk a hiker's good friend. A hefty dose can go into
a number of trail foods, and I make it a practice always to add
extra. Instant pudding that requires ²/₃ cup, for instance, gets a
full cup instead.

White (or Cream) Sauce

is a regular protein source at home, and a respectable facsimile
can be made for trail use. It incorporates a grocery store item
called Butter Buds, an all-natural powder with the flavor of butter

(but little nutritional value). A box equaling the flavor of 2 pounds of butter contains eight foil packets and costs about $1.40. Here's a backpacking adaptation of the product's Basic White Sauce:

At home (for 6 to 8 servings), bag together:

1 packet Butter Buds	⅔ cup instant dry milk
3 tablespoons flour (whole wheat is richest)	¼ teaspoon salt
	pepper

In camp: Blend dry mix with 2 cups water, stir and heat slowly until thickened.

Uses for this adaptable sauce are limitless:

- Add tuna and cooked veggies for a rich main dish
- Add chunked sausage and cheese and serve over English muffins for breakfast
- Stir in canned chunked chicken and reconstituted freeze-dried peas and serve over hot biscuits
- Stir in grated cheese and add the sauce to pasta
- Transform into chowder with canned minced clams, finely diced and sautéed potato and onion, and a dab of margarine

Berley Lakes Bulgur

This meatless main dish provides a big dose of protein at a mere 34¢ a serving. The secrets are complementary protein—bulgur (parboiled cracked wheat with a delicious nutty flavor) and soy grits together yield complete protein such as found in meat— and a willingness to shop at more than one source. The bulgur, soy grits and dried veggies come from the natural foods store, and the other ingredients from the grocery store. The veggies, of course, could also be ones you've grown and dehydrated yourself, lowering the price even more. Or, in all but the hottest weather, some fresh veggies that travel well.

If you like, on occasions when thrift isn't a goal, meat can be added to this recipe in several forms: canned, precooked and frozen hamburger, freeze-dried chunks.

(for 2 or 3 servings)

Bag together:

¾ cup bulgur
¼ cup soy grits
a handful of dried zucchini slices
a handful of other dried veggies
1 tablespoon dried chopped onion

2 tablespoons dried parsley flakes
1 cube (or 1 teaspoon) beef bouillon
pepper

Wrap separately: ½ cup slivered almonds. Label with directions: "Add all but nuts to 3½ cups boiling water; simmer, covered, 15 minutes, adding water if needed. Top with nuts."

Peanut Butter Spread

is so versatile it will work its way into many parts of the day's eating. Carry this high-protein spread in a bottom-filling plastic tube and use it as a topping for sturdy crackers or bread, celery, even big dried fruit chunks. It includes the nutritional wallop of milk without altering a basic nutty-rich flavor.

Mix equal parts peanut butter and molasses (or honey for a subtler taste but fewer nutrients), then work in as much instant dry milk as possible. To make the mixture spreadable, blend in a small amount of soft margarine.

Candy is a convenient trail snack, but costs dearly, is loaded with sugar and most has little protein. An excellent substitute you can whip up at home in minutes is a variation on the Peanut Butter Spread theme. In addition to plenty of protein, you'll get calcium and iron from the molasses and B vitamins from the wheat germ.

Molasses Marbles

(MAKES ABOUT 2 DOZEN)

A 2-marble serving costs about 14¢, half the price of a candy bar. Mix together:

½ cup molasses
½ cup peanut butter

¾ cup instant dry milk
¾ cup toasted wheat germ

Roll small balls in one of these: chopped nuts, sesame seeds, coconut flakes, sunflower seed kernels.

Sesame Honeys

Your own delicious penny-wise answer to commercial wafers that cost 35¢ each. Buy seeds and nuts in bulk and toast in a 350° F oven for 15 minutes, spread in a thin layer.
Mix:

2 cups toasted sesame seeds   ½ cup chopped nuts (peanuts, almonds, walnuts)

In a large frying pan, combine ½ cup each honey and packed brown sugar, ¼ teaspoon salt and ¾ teaspoon ground cinnamon. Bring to a boil over medium heat, stirring constantly; cook for 2 minutes. Remove pan from heat and quickly stir in seeds and nuts, mixing well. Turn into a buttered 9-by-14-inch pan. With the back of a spoon, press mixture firmly and evenly down. Let cool at room temperature for 15 minutes, then cut into bars. When very firm (about 2 hours), wrap in plastic wrap.

Home-cooked meats

offer an economical and welcome "real food" taste to backpackers who aren't quite ready to forsake meat altogether on their jaunts. They can be the basis for many a quick one-pot dinner. Uncooked meats, of course, are too messy to fuss with in the trail kitchen. And besides, they're too subject to spoilage to be safe.

One solution is to precook, then freeze the meat at home. Carry it well insulated in your pack and use within 4 or 5 days (sooner in very hot weather).

With a hike on the calendar, I'll frequently serve pot roast or round steak during the week or two before, allowing for plenty of leftovers. Bite-sized pieces go into a plastic bag (often with some of the dish's sauce), then into the freezer until I pack for the trip. (A note also gets pinned to my pack so I don't forget: "+ boots, car lunch and freezer stuff!")

Another thrifty way to have meat in the backcountry kitchen

is to precook and freeze seasoned hamburger. I buy 5-pound tubes of ground beef when they're on special and cook up enough for several trips.

Sometimes I blend in chopped onion, garlic powder, Worcestershire sauce, pepper and dry mustard before browning the meat. If I want a meat-and-gravy result in camp, I stir in bouillon and flour as the meat browns, then add water in camp (for each pound of meat: 1 bouillon cube, 3 tablespoons flour, 1 cup water). Voilà! Gravy!

You can expand this versatile base into dozens of main dishes, depending on how you season it. A few examples:

- In camp, add vegetables and water to the basic mix, cook for a stew, and top with dumplings (page 74).
- Prepare a meat sauce with chili powder, garlic, onion and tomato sauce at home, then heat in camp and serve in flour tortillas as burritos. Grate cheese and chop fresh onion to top the meat filling, then cap with sour cream sauce and a dab of salsa (carried in a film cannister).
- Use in One-Liners (pages 83–92) wherever beef is called for.

Singular Sausage

costs less than half as much as most you buy, and is scrumptious! Custom tailor the seasonings to your tastes, and vary them from batch to batch. Your unique sausage costs about $1 a roll and keeps several days without refrigeration. Refrigerate or freeze for long-term storage.

5 pounds ground beef
5 teaspoons Morton's Tender Quik Curing Salt (with the spices in most grocery stores)
2 teaspoons coarsely ground pepper

2 teaspoons garlic salt
2 teaspoons mustard seed
1 teaspoon hickory-smoked salt

Mix all the spices together. Crumble the meat and thoroughly mix in the spices with your hands. Cover and refrigerate for 24 hours. On the second day: mix again, refrigerate for another 24 hours. On the third day: shape into five rolls about 1½ inches in diameter. Put on a metal rack 2 inches apart and bake for 8 hours at 150° F, turning every 2 hours.

FRESH VEGETABLES IN SEASON

are a bargain (especially from your garden). Use them on short trips when some heavier, bulkier provisions are acceptable, or on one of your first few days of a longer trip. The tomatoes for this quick and colorful dish should be packed carefully so that they won't be squashed (maybe inside a cook kit?)

Fresh Veggie Medley
(2 BIG SERVINGS)

At home: Pack a medium-sized yellow summer squash, 2 medium tomatoes, 3 or 4 small onions and a slab of cheese. Havarti, Cheddar and Monterey Jack all go well with the vegetable flavors. *In camp:* Cut the veggies into big chunks and cook gently in an inch or so of water, covered, until barely tender—6 to 8 minutes. Sliver on some cheese, mix it in and add more to the top. Cover and let stand off the stove just until the cheese melts. A sprinkling of sesame seeds tastes great and adds a bit more protein as well as textural variety.

17

~~~~~

Emergency Foods

*I*n some corner of your pack you should *always* carry an emergency food supply; let's hope it's never needed. The foods you choose for this sealed packet should be ones that keep well for long periods (I change mine every several months, just to be on the safe side). They'll be lightweight and compact, and provide a high level of energy for activity and body warmth.

Don't make a mistake I did in early hiking days—carrying a favorite food. The rock candy tucked in with my emergency supplies was too tempting; it got eaten the third day out! Some folks go to the other extreme and pack dog food, knowing they won't eat it unless times are really tough.

Most emergency foods should be edible as is without further preparation or, at most, require only a little water. If you are in an emergency situation, you may be without fuel or easily available water, and your mobility may be limited by injury. With these considerations in mind, you might take:

- Mealpack bar (complete protein, 450 calories, less than 4 ounces)
- Jerky
- Meat or bacon bar (2 ounces, precooked, condensed)
- Dried fruits
- Pemmican (page 105)
- Logan Bread (page 104)
- Condensed mincemeat bar
- Bouillon or soup powder
- Hard candy
- Gumdrops or jelly beans
- Kendall mint cake (outdoor store)
- A dry cheese such as smoked Gouda (paraffin-coated)
- Nuts
- A trail mix of nuts and raisins

Also put in some candles and matches wrapped to stay dry.

18

A Touch of the Wild

*L*earning and using a few wild plants along with your hiking food adds exciting variety to your diet, builds knowledge that could be used in a survival situation and puts you very directly in touch with the land you have come to be part of. The study of wild edibles is exciting, and will give you a whole new way of being part of wilderness life.

Using a plant respectfully is really just a specialized part of becoming friendly with growing things, learning their names, their looks, their growth stages, their home territories. And that kind of friendliness repays you so fully for the efforts you put into it! You walk through the woods or desert and know you are meeting a lot of friends on the way.

It is not usually appropriate (or possible) to try to live solely off the land, but careful, respectful use of plants is all right. Some plants, of course, can hardly be "used up" . . . eating all the sweet wild strawberries you want will still leave enough for the critters, and the plant will continue to grow. Catching a few trout for breakfast will not seriously deplete the supply. Nor will brewing a cup of fresh mint tea.

But when you eat roots and bulbs, this can limit the future growth of the plant. The bulbs of the glacier and avalanche lilies can be eaten either raw or cooked, but because they are so sparse and beautiful, they really *never* should be used. Wild onions add zest to stew or soup, but be sure there are several growing together before you dig any bulbs. Those onions won't grow back next year! Snipping a few onion tops from a thick patch obviously isn't a depleting practice.

A good approach to learning and using edible plants is to familiarize yourself with a dozen or more of the most common ones in your hiking areas, rather than trying to learn so many all at once that you get confused and discouraged. Also learn the *poisonous* plants you might encounter, since eating even a small amount of some (such as water hemlock) is enough to cause serious illness or even death.

Generally, plants are safer cooked than raw. Some plants that are basically edible are also poisonous unless prepared at certain growth stages or in certain ways. Bracken fern in its mature stages is toxic in large quantities, and most varieties of acorns must be leached of their tannic acid before the ground meal is safe to use. (Then it is absolutely delicious in foods like biscuits!) Many poisonous plants bear a close resemblance to others that are safe. Poisonous water hemlock looks much like cow parsnip as well as several other edible plants.

A FEW BASIC RULES ABOUT EATING WILD THINGS

Be SAFE.

- Pick what you *know* is edible and know how to use.
- Use soon after gathering.
- Eat sparingly of a new food.
- The fact that animals and birds can safely eat a plant does *not* mean that humans necessarily can.

Be CONSERVING.

- Pick only abundant plants still able to grow.
- Spread your harvesting over a wide area: a few leaves from each of many plants, for instance.

Many good books about wild edibles are available, usually dealing with particular regions. One I've found especially helpful is Donald R. Kirk's *Wild Edible Plants of the Western United States* (Naturegraph Publishers). Several features of this and any good reference book are:

- Clear, concise information about each plant (illustration, scientific and common names, description, habitat and distribution, preparation and uses)
- Compact form, easily tucked into a pack
- Firm, explicit information about the *poisonous* plants in the region, knowledge of which is a *must* if you plan to eat *anything* wild

A valuable feature of Mr. Kirk's book is found at the end, where there is a "nutshell index of plant food uses" (and also an index of plant uses other than food, such as for medicines, dyes, fibers, soap, implements). The food index lists by reference number the plants that fit into many use categories, such as: beverages, cereals, emergency, greens, nuts, oils, roots, salads, soups, wines. For my own quick field use and to share with classes, I abstracted from this index a brief list of some common edible plants of my hiking areas by plant name and use. This list got me over that frustrating stage of learning where I could identify the plant but couldn't remember what to do with it.

For example, one section of my list looks like this:

TEAS

(If using leaves, they should be either fresh or dried, not in between.)

- Hemlock (needles)
- Douglas fir (needles)
- chicory (ground dried roots)
- Scotch broom (roasted seeds)
- yarrow (entire plant)
- strawberry (leaves)

Learning about the plants where you hike, you might use your favorite reference books to compile a similar list. This practice is a real help in solidifying the knowledge you may already have about wild edibles and in sparking your eagerness to learn more.

When you plan to work some wild foods into a trip's meals, consider tucking a few of these supplies into your pack:

for fish: cooking oil, margarine, a whole lemon or lemon pepper, a bag of seasoned cornmeal for coating

for cooked greens: margarine, salt and pepper, sesame meal, cold bacon drippings for a quick sauté

for wild cobblers: a bag of topping mix (page 97) and perhaps a sweetener for the fruit—white or brown sugar, whole or dehydrated honey

for tea: whole or dehydrated honey, sugar

for salads: lemon juice or oil-and-vinegar dressing

Once a year or so when I know certain "tea" plants will be abundant on a hike, I'll pack plastic bags to hold a large quantity of each herb gathered—usually yarrow, mint, sage. Then one of the first projects on my return home is to dry these pungent plants and package them singly or in combinations. They make unique and treasured Christmas gifts, carrying with them the aura of summer pleasures in grand places.

Some of my cherished wild foods memories are:

- brewing wine from the blue elderberries on a friend's farm
- a spring search of fern "fiddleheads" to serve with Sunday dinner
- hours spent leaching tannin from acorns, then drying and grinding the meal into flour
- a marvel—the complex design and crisp taste of sliced young cattail shoots
- with a friend, patiently gathering Scotch broom pods on a hot late-summer day; later roasting and grinding the seeds for an exotic coffee
- cooking up gifts of jam from blackberries and wild mint
- the delicate aroma of my daughter's clover blossom tea
- midwinter thoughts of a dear friend, as her gift of dried yellow chanterelle mushrooms bubble in my snow-camp stewpot

19

~~~~~

Home-Dried Foods

H ome-dried edibles are a natural for the backcountry, meeting all the tests of a good trail food: lightweight, compact, sturdy, tasty, easy to fix, nonperishable, nutritious, inexpensive. Compared with commercial dried foods, your own are even lighter, less perishable and tastier!

Versatility also counts for a lot (like the bandana with a dozen uses), and these foods can fill many niches in your wilderness menus. By drying your own, you can tailor the shapes, sizes, blends and seasonings to turn out a variety of offerings you'd never be able to buy: herbed mushrooms, a batch of jerky with several different flavors, tomato or strawberry slices, plum sauce, thin peach slices that rehydrate in a minute in oatmeal.

Creative, fun and easy to learn, home food drying on even a small scale without a food dryer can produce an endless range of items to work into your meal plans.

Most home-dried products weigh one-third or less their original weight (carrots and tomatoes only one-tenth) and are one-third to one-half their original size. When properly dried and stored, foods keep several seasons. They're healthful, lacking additives and preservatives. More food value is retained than by methods of preservation using higher heat or water.

Commercially available dried foods usually cost at least double the do-it-yourself kind. Savings are even greater if you have access to a garden, U-pick produce, bargain prices for large quantities or trades.

If you've priced food dryers and decided the investment of $100 and up is too much, please reconsider. There are other alternatives: sun, oven, a homemade unit, or a joint purchase with hiking friends or neighbors.

Once you start, the satisfactions of the art and the products that reward you will convince you it was a smart move. If you use it much at all, even a middle-priced dryer soon pays for itself.

A dryer can be used year-round, since something is available every month (pineapple, mushrooms, herbs, meat and poultry, nuts, the frozen berries you were too busy to dry in July). Mine does another regular job, turning out a big monthly batch of yogurt in a mere 3 hours. Besides filling your own pack, home-dried foods make treasured gifts for outdoor friends and home snackers.

SELECTED DRIED DELIGHTS:
AN ENTICING SAMPLING OF THE
GREAT THINGS YOU CAN TURN OUT

- Dry spaghetti sauce as leather; reconstitute in camp by simmering big pieces in water and stirring.
- Combine dried fruit bits with instant pudding, pancakes, biscuits, cereals.
- Bag fruit bits, nuts and spices together for an original trail mix.
- Make soup blends from dried veggies and spices (look at soup packets in stores for suggested ingredients).
- Sweet and versatile pineapple chunks: snack on them as is, blend with other flavors in stewed fruits, add to a sweet-and-sour dinner pot of rice, ham, green pepper and sauce.

- Unusual appetizers: dried tomato or zucchini chips with a dip made in the bag from sour-cream sauce mix and herbs or onion soup powder

NOW ON TO THE BASICS

Drying (also called *dehydration*) is simply preservation by the gradual, gentle removal of moisture from fresh foods. The process has been used for centuries.

Drying requires two equally important conditions: (a) a fairly constant low-range heat source (90° to 145° F); and (b) adequate air circulation to carry off the moisture extracted.

In areas with many warm, dry days, it can be accomplished in the sun, as long as foods are protected from insects, birds, cats and dogs. Oven drying works for some, provided a temperature below 150° F can be maintained. A dryer you build or buy gives controlled heat, adequate air circulation, increased drying space and it works 24 hours a day.

Purchased dryers of good quality cost between $100 and $200 and certainly make sense if you plan to dry more than small amounts of food. When friends share the cost, use and products of a dryer, it's even more economical.

Basic carpentry skills and $60 to $80 are all that are needed to build a functional dryer from plans found in many books on drying or available from your local agricultural extension service.

WHEN SHOPPING FOR A DRYER OR PLANS TO BUILD ONE WITH, LOOK FOR:

- The most convenient size and shape for your home. (There are square and round, counter-top and floor models. My Excalibur looks like a microwave oven.)
- A large enough capacity, but not larger than you can manage. I found my first dryer, with 10 square feet, too small. My present, with 16 square feet, is just right ... not too much space to fill at one time, but large

enough to take advantage of a bumper tomato crop.
The price difference between small and medium units
isn't much.

- A thermostatically controlled range of 90° to 145° F,
  with a safety cutoff in case of overheating.
- A fan that blows a good strong current of air through or
  across all trays.
- Easy-clean, nonsagging, nontoxic trays (many are coated
  with Teflon, a real plus).

How long does it take?

The process takes from a few hours to many hours depending
on method, density and moisture content of the fresh food and
size of the pieces.

Generally, drying is slowest in the sun, somewhat faster in a
dryer with just air vents and no fan, faster yet in an oven (whose
door must be propped open a bit to allow moist air to escape),
fastest in a dryer with both heat source and fan.

The quickest foods to dry (3 to 6 hours) are herbs, paper-
thin slices of fruits or vegetables, and thin fruit leathers. Longest-
drying (up to 48 hours or more) are thick chunks of pineapple,
raisins, uncut prunes, and unpeeled halves of heavy fruits such
as pears and peaches. In between are jerky, sliced fruits and
vegetables and most fruit leathers.

Must foods be pretreated before drying?

Opinions vary on the necessity and worth of pretreatments, and
many people use none at all. If you plan to use dried foods within
a year, are careful in drying, packaging and storing and don't
place a high priority on appearance, try skipping this step and
see if the results suit you.

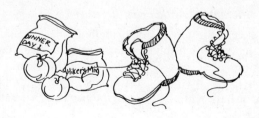

GENERAL TECHNIQUES

One of the most appealing things about drying is its lack of precision. There are a few basic principles to heed, but also much leeway in the actual procedures. Unlike regular cooking, it's hard to botch up the drying so badly that the product is unusable.

Preheat your dryer for about 15 minutes, since the temperature will drop a bit when you load it with trays of fresh foods. Use choice, ripe fruits and crisp vegetables. Handle foods quickly. Wash, peel or not as you choose, cut out any bruises and bad spots, and cut the food into pieces of fairly uniform size. (A vegetable slicer, salad shredder, food processor or similar tool is helpful here.) Generally, pieces shouldn't exceed ½ inch in thickness. The thinner and smaller the pieces, the faster they'll dry.

Arrange food loosely on trays, without crowding or overlapping pieces. This will allow air to circulate freely and carry off moisture. A frequent cause of spoilage in the drying process is impatience; crowded foods keep the temperature low and air moist, and mold can develop.

Drying foods shrink and can be consolidated after a few hours, leaving room for more fresh trays to be added (always toward the top of the dryer, since warm, moist air rises).

Foods that are very juicy and likely to drip can be placed on pieces of plastic cut smaller than the trays for the first few hours. This impedes the air flow, so some people prefer simply to place a piece of drip-catching foil in the bottom of the dryer.

When drying foods whose finished form will be very small (grated citrus rind, flaked tuna, shredded carrots and such), it's helpful to cover trays with same-size rectangles of nylon net or tulle. This facilitates gathering and removing the dried food. The net can be washed with the family laundry. Some dryers build in this feature; mine has removable Teflon screens, a touch of genius!

Can different foods be dried together?

Yes, except the most strong-smelling ones (onion, garlic, peppers, jerky) which might transfer odors. So if you have small quantities of several different things to dry, process them all together. You may want just enough cabbage and carrots for a salad, or have a bunch of overripe bananas that will make good leather.

What temperature do I use?

Temperatures at which foods are ideally dried vary considerably, but by using your common sense and paying attention to what is happening to the foods, you'll soon get away from rigid adherence to rules.

In general, herbs and other leafy green things need a relatively low temperature (90° to 100° F); fruits dry successfully at 125° to 140° F; vegetables, meat and fish, all more prone to spoil, require a higher temperature of 130° to 145° F. If you buy a dryer, follow the temperature guidelines that accompany it.

It does no good to try to speed up the drying process by using a higher temperature than recommended. What happens then is called case hardening: The outside will dry hard and tight, and inside moisture will be trapped. Case-hardened food is edible, of course, but won't keep long because the high moisture content lets spoilage organisms grow.

How do I know when foods are dry enough?

Take a piece or two out, let cool a few minutes, then bend. Most fruits should be leathery and pliable, most vegetables hard and brittle, leafy green things crackly dry with no sign of moisture.

SOME SPECIAL TECHNIQUES

- For trail use, it's best to cut most vegetables intended for cooking into fairly small pieces before drying. They'll rehydrate and cook more quickly.
- I frequently dry a batch of fruit in several forms, for varied uses. Apples, for instance, get this treatment: some rings, some slices, some leather (with varied spices and maybe some nuts), the rest shredded (the basis for instant applesauce).
- Vegetables in different forms are useful, too. When I dry carrots, some are shredded (for salads), some are long thin strips made with a vegetable peeler (for soup, stew and to cook plain).
- Mushrooms, tomato slices, summer squashes and greens such as spinach will rehydrate in minutes, a plus for camp use.

- Small things such as peas, blueberries, shredded vegetables or fruits need occasional stirring to expose all surfaces.
- To retard oxidation and darkening of apples, peaches and similar fruits, dip first in lemon, orange or pineapple juice. This step isn't *necessary,* just an option.
- To speed the drying of grapes, whole prunes and figs, crack their skins by quickly blanching in boiling water, then rinse in cold water, blot dry.
- If drying is uneven, turn the trays 180° midway in the process.

MAKING AND USING JERKY

Jerky can be made from almost any *lean* meat or poultry (not lamb or pork). Round steak and roast work well, but don't pay extra for choice grades; tenderness doesn't count! Partially freeze the leanest meat you can find (4 pounds makes 1 pound of jerky), then cut it into strips no thicker than ¼ inch. Slice *with* the grain for a chewy texture or *across* the grain for more tender jerky.

Now, use either dry seasonings or a marinade (suggestions follow) to load the meat with flavor—natural, smoky, hot or spicy. Sprinkle or pour your choice of seasonings over layers of meat strips in a bowl, stir to coat well, cover and marinate for 1 hour at room temperature or 6 to 12 hours in the refrigerator. Stir occasionally during this time to distribute flavors.

Drain the marinated meat before spreading nonoverlapping slices on trays to dry (save the marinade in the refrigerator or freezer to use again; it's expensive). If you've used a variety of flavorings, label each row with a strip of freezer tape, which you can later transfer to the storage container. Dry at 145° F until hard but not brittle (usually 8 to 12 hours). Use a paper towel to blot up any fat that appears.

Try these *dry seasonings* singly or in blends (making notes of what you use, so that you can repeat successes): salt, pepper, lemon pepper, hickory-smoked salt, onion or celery salt, chili powder, garlic powder, onion powder, cumin, curry powder, teriyaki sauce mix powder, pickling spices, salad dressing mix.

Brew up a *marinade:*

Teriyaki

1 cup soy sauce
1 tablespoon brown sugar
1 clove garlic, minced

1 teaspoon ground ginger
½ teaspoon ground pepper

Smoky

2 tablespoons liquid smoke
1 teaspoon garlic powder

½ teaspoon ground pepper

Tangy

1 cup red wine
2 tablespoons Worcestershire
  sauce
½ teaspoon Tabasco sauce

1 teaspoon garlic salt
½ teaspoon ground pepper
½ teaspoon paprika

Far East

1 cup soy sauce
1 tablespoon dry sherry

1 clove garlic, minced
2 tablespoons sesame seeds

Teriyaki Turkey Jerky

Along with making my annual mincemeat pie and a dryer load
of spiced cranberry leather, Thanksgiving includes another tra-
dition for me—drying a batch of these exotic tidbits. I bake a
turkey larger than needed for the feast, so that there'll be plenty
left over to transform into jerky for snow-camping trips. Occasionally the freezer still holds a packet or two when summer's
first hikes are planned.

Cut cooked turkey into slices ¼ inch thick; soak for 15 minutes
or longer in bottled teriyaki sauce, stirring now and then to coat
all surfaces.

Drain, then place slices without overlapping on trays. (If using an oven, place slices on cake racks set on rimmed cookie sheets.) Dry for 4 to 6 hours in the dryer at 145° F, or in the oven set at its lowest temperature (prop the door open). When done, the slices should feel hard and dry, but not brittle.

Drying Fish

Small fish can be dried whole, but large ones should have the fat and skin removed, be fileted and cut into cubes about ½ by 1 inch. Shrimp, crab and clams don't usually need slicing. Fish must be dried *very* firm, with no soft spots, at 145° F.

"Smoked" Fish Treats

For an easy delicacy that tastes smoked, start with either tiny fresh shrimp or pieces of salmon (remove skin and bones, cut salmon into pieces no thicker than ½ inch). Put fish chunks into a bowl, pour on soy sauce, stir and let stand for 15 minutes. Then drain and spread to dry until very firm. These treats cost half as much as commercially smoked salmon.

Tuna

Occasionally I drain and dry water-packed tuna to use on trips when very lightweight foods are needed.

What can I do with all that jerky and fish?

Jerky has many uses besides the traditional eating out of hand as snacks or with lunch. It makes an elegant breakfast in bed and a delightful addition to soups and one-pot dinner dishes. For cooking, break into small pieces, because no matter how long you cook it, jerky will never be tender again! As your pot simmers, the rich marinade or spice flavors will be released.

For pepping up scrambled eggs or hash browns, cut the original slices very thin (⅛ inch) so that the jerky will crumble easily. To flavor corncakes or biscuits, soak these crumbles for a few minutes first if there's time. Carry chived cream cheese in a plastic tube and squirt a bit on jerky strips for a gourmet appetizer.

Fruit Leather

Fresh fruits are heavy and squashable on the trail, but you can carry their rich flavors and nourishment with you in the form of leather, which is simply fruit puree spread in a puddle and dried to a pliable, nonsticky state. Leathers are easy to carry and eat and are aesthetically pleasing. Hold a piece of peach or strawberry leather up to the sunlight and you have a woodsy stained-glass window!

Leathers are available in stores, but yours cost a fraction of the going price and can be in any exotic flavors you dream up . . . banana–nut, spiced pear, strawberry–rhubarb!

If you happen upon free or bargain-priced fruit, puree it all, dry what you can at the time and freeze the rest to make leathers when your dryer isn't busy.

Skip the puree step with bananas if there's plenty of room in the freezer and you need to save time. Pop the bunches of fruit in as is. The skins will turn black, but the insides stay perfect, ready to thaw and use in any way that requires mashing. This tactic let me take advantage of a terrific bargain just before a long hike, when I had little drying time. I bought 82 pounds of bananas, baked bread by the ovenful, dried one load of "chips" and froze the rest of my bonanza. I'll make leather when the dust settles this fall.

Leathers can be made from single fruits or combinations of two or more, sweetened with honey or coconut if you like (though they usually don't need any help), made tart with lemon juice or grated peel or flavored with spices, vanilla or almond extract. Be creative and experiment, tasting as you blend. If it tastes good in the blender, the finished product will be delicious.

Leathers keep for a month or more at room temperature, about 4 months in the refrigerator, and a year or longer in the freezer.

Basic instructions for making leathers:

1. Use very ripe fruit. Over-the-hill bananas are great!
   Wash; cut out any bruised spots. Don't bother to peel apples, pears, peaches and such.

2. With a blender, food grinder or food processor, reduce fruits to a smooth pulp. Don't add any liquid unless it's needed for blending action. If you do, use water, juice or cider. Some fruits blend better if cooked a little first (gently, in one of these liquids): cranberries, rhubarb, apples.

3. The puree should be about like thick applesauce. If thickening is needed, add apple (high in natural pectin), wheat germ, chopped nuts, pectin or unflavored gelatin. I prefer to use combinations of fruit that result in the right thickness . . . such as berry/apple, banana/peach. You may want to strain some of the seeds from berry purees.

4. Pour puree no thicker than 1/4 inch onto plastic (such as bread wrappers) and dry at about 135° F until you can peel the sheet off cleanly. The time required varies from 6 to 14 hours, depending on consistency of the puree. Don't overdry; it should be chewy but not stiff.

5. Store rolled in plastic wrap. *Label!* Pear and apple leather look alike, as do plum and cranberry.

Here are some tasty leather combinations to get you started. As you experiment with fruits, spices and other additions, make notes of blends you especially like so that you can reproduce them.

- cranberry/unpeeled orange/chopped dates
- peach/banana/chopped walnuts/ginger
- pear/apple/mint extract
- apricot/pineapple
- pear/chopped almonds/nutmeg
- apple/chopped filberts/cinnamon/allspice
- banana/pineapple/sesame seeds
- cherry/coconut
- apple/pineapple/coconut
- plum/apple/cinnamon
- apricot/chopped almonds
- peach/blueberry
- strawberry/rhubarb (softened first by cooking)
- mincemeat (alone, or with apple)
- pumpkin pie filling/apple/pumpkin pie spice
- pear/raisins/ginger

Fruit leather is a classic piece of backpacking "gear," serving multiple functions:

- Carry whole rolls or cut them into bite-sized lengths and pack in a *snack* bag. If you have several kinds, gather a variety.
- When you want *jam* to top muffins, bread or crackers, tear off a piece of leather.
- You can reverse the drying process on the trail and turn leather into a delicious *sauce* for breakfast or dessert. Just heat water, add big pieces of leather and stir as it reconstitutes.
- A really elegant dessert is *filled leather rolls,* which look like miniature jelly rolls. Fix them at home before a trip. Unroll leather and spread with either softened cream cheese or peanut butter, leaving a 1-inch margin. Roll up the leather, then cut into bit-sized pieces. You might want to reassemble the roll and carry it in a cardboard tube.

PACKAGING DRIED FOODS
FOR TRAIL USE

When your dried foods are headed for the wild places, what do you do with them as they come out of the dryer? Correct storage is essential to preservation; foods that have been dried right can be lost in storage if just a few basic rules are ignored.

Any method of storage you choose needs to keep out air, moisture, bugs and light. Several things work well: for home storage, glass jars (dark ones are best) with a good seal; sealable plastic bags with the extra air squeezed out; plastic containers with tight-sealing lids.

Resealable plastic bags are handiest and most compact for hikers. Some people feel they are somewhat permeable by moisture and can transmit a "plastic" taste to foods stored for more than a few weeks. The bags made for use with home bag-sealing machines are much better for long-term storage of foods you'll open just once and use. If foods are stored in containers that don't exclude light, the bags or jars can be put into paper bags or into cans with tight lids for home storage.

Bugs and mice find these tasty foods appealing, so if you store plastic bags in cupboards, gather them first into another, rigid container.

All dried foods need to be kept in a cool (60° F or less), dark place. The drier the food, the longer it keeps, so don't expect relatively moist fruit leather or pineapple chunks to last for years, the way brittle vegetables will. Shelf life can be extended greatly by putting dried foods in the refrigerator or freezer. Store foods in usable quantities so you won't be opening packages frequently, letting moisture in.

Let foods cool before packaging. During the first 2 weeks of storage, check the packages every few days to see if the food is as dry as when you sealed it. If there's more obvious moisture, return the food to the dryer for an hour or more, then repackage. By checking early, spoilage can be avoided and the food rescued. If you find mold, remove it, dry the remainder of the food longer, and try again. Widespread mold or an "off" smell indicate that the food has spoiled beyond saving.

Foods can be stored separately or in combinations, so think ahead to how you'll use them on the trail and bag mixed fruits for cobbler, vegetable blends for soup or main dishes.

Sometimes the package later doubles as a soaking or serving bowl. Whatever the packaging mode, label *everything!* Many foods look alike, and many don't bear much resemblance to their fresh state.

If a food has some special significance, I sometimes add a note: "Don's Hood River pears," "red huckleberries picked with Shirley." This adds to the pleasure of using it later.

Foods should be dried and stored in different sized pieces for various kinds of trail use: big fruit chunks for snacks, smaller for fast cooking in fruit soup, *very* small or thin for adding to cereal or pancake batter, powdered (after drying) or finely chopped fruits for trail shake mix, powdered vegetables for instant soup mix. Remember: smaller pieces rehydrate and cook faster.

MORE DRIED DELIGHTS

Herbed Mushroom Gems

(APPETIZERS FOR 4 TO 6)

Into a big bowl at home, slice 1 pound fresh mushrooms ¼ inch thick.
Combine:

½ teaspoon each salt, sesame meal and oregano

¼ teaspoon each onion salt and garlic salt

Sprinkle seasoning mixture over mushroom slices, stirring gently to coat. Now spread the slices on trays to dry at 120° F until crisp (4 to 6 hours). In an oven, use the lowest heat setting possible and prop the door open.

Garden Soup Mix

(SERVES 4 TO 6)

At home, mix and bag:

1 cup dried and crushed spinach leaves

2 tablespoons instant potato flakes

2 tablespoons mixed dried and powdered vegetable bits

1 tablespoon Butter Buds

2 teaspoons (or 2 cubes) chicken bouillon

¼ teaspoon dried rosemary pepper

In camp: Stir mix into 3 cups boiling water. Let sit a few minutes, then stir again, adding more hot water if too thick.

Green and Orange Salad

(6 SERVINGS)

At home, pack together in a 1-gallon ziplock bag:

1½ cups dried shredded carrots

1½ cups dried shredded cabbage

¾ cup raisins

½ cup small dried pineapple bits

Mix dressing and carry in a small leakproof plastic bottle:

2 teaspoons each sugar, vine-   ½ teaspoon salt
gar, vegetable oil

In camp: Add enough cold water to cover the dried mix in the bag. Seal, knead a bit to moisten everything and soak for 30 minutes. Drain off any excess liquid (add it to the soup pot to save nutrients). Shake dressing, add to bag, mix well and serve.

Apple Slaw
(6 SERVINGS)

At home, pack together in a 1-gallon ziplock bag:

2 cups dried shredded cabbage   ½ cup dark raisins
1 cup dried diced unpeeled ap-
ples (red are best)

Mix dressing and carry in a small leakproof plastic bottle:

1 tablespoon each lemon juice,   ½ teaspoon salt
sugar and vegetable oil

In camp: Add enough cold water to cover dried mix in bag. Seal, knead a bit to moisten everything and soak for 30 minutes. Drain off any excess liquid. Shake dressing, add to bag, mix well and serve.

Lebanese Tabbouli Salad

(SERVES 4)

At home, pack together in a 1-quart ziplock bag:

1 cup bulgur
a big handful of broken dried
  tomato slices
¼ cup dried parsley flakes

3 tablespoons dried leeks OR 2
  tablespoons dried onion
1½ teaspoons dried mint OR 1
  tablespoon fresh from the
  wilds

Mix dressing and carry in a small leakproof plastic bottle:

3 tablespoons olive or vegetable oil

2 tablespoons lemon juice

In camp: Add 3 cups cold water to dried mix in its bag; soak
for 45 to 60 minutes. When bulgur is softened (but not mushy . . . a
little crunch is good), drain off any excess liquid (into the soup
pot). Shake dressing, add to bag, mix well and serve.

Chunky Strawberry–Rhubarb Sauce

(SERVES 4)

Dry rhubarb in ¼-inch diagonal slices. Dry strawberries (big
ones are best) in ⅓-inch slices.
At home, pack in one bag:

1½ cups dried rhubarb slices

Pack in another bag:

½ cup dried strawberry slices
3 tablespoons dehydrated
  honey

¼ teaspoon ground nutmeg

In camp: Simmer rhubarb in water to cover until almost tender.
Add strawberries and honey, stirring gently to dissolve honey.
Heat just until strawberries are soft.

Hot Fruit Soup

(SERVES 4)

A splendid dessert! You might sometime want to save half for breakfast the next morning.

At home, bag together:

2 cups mixed dried fruits, diced	1 teaspoon ground cinnamon

Pack in another bag:

¼ cup quick-cooking tapioca	½ cup instant dry milk

In camp: Simmer fruits in water to cover until almost tender. Add another cup of water and blend in the milk/tapioca. Cook gently, stirring, until the tapioca becomes transparent.

Apple Snackle

(MAKES 3 CUPS)

Stir together:

1 cup dried chopped apples	½ cup walnut pieces
1 cup dark raisins	½ cup brown sugar
½ cup chopped dried dates	1 teaspoon ground cinnamon

Variation: Use chopped dried pears instead of apples and add ¼ teaspoon ground nutmeg.

Almost any *favorite casserole-type main dish* can be cooked and then dried, for reconstituting on the trail. This is useful when: (a) the recipe is too complicated for adapting as a one-liner (see pages 82–92); (b) foods need to be very lightweight; (c) you want variety.

One summer trip in Oregon mountains we savored a visiting friend's Ratatouille on rice, dried in New York and brought cross-country for the occasion!

20

Winter Camp Cookery

*N*othing is more satisfying to body and soul than a hot, delicious meal in a snug snow camp! But it's often a bit tricky to achieve.

Picture a winter camp, your home for a night in the course of a weekend or several days or weeks of snow journeying. The special conditions you may find in this setting (as opposed to those of "dirt camping") have a direct bearing on how you plan, pack and eat the food that is brought along to sustain and please you.

Depending on the time of year, part of the country, type of terrain and current weather, snow camping may be done in conditions that range from mild to severe. But no matter when or where you snow camp, it is wise to assume that you'll be challenged by weather and other factors that call forth all the resourcefulness you can muster.

Temperatures are usually cold enough to numb the hands wielding cooking pots; inactive feet can turn into icebergs while they stand around waiting for meals. Cooks are bundled up in bulky clothes that get in the way of swift, easy motion. Mittens limit the dexterity of hands trying to light stoves, manage spoons and pots, open food packages . . . but bare hands hardly function at all in nippy air, and certainly invite frostbite. The liquids in unprotected water bottles can freeze.

In addition to cold, a major challenge in winter camp cooking is the frequent scarcity of liquid water. Yes, it's all around in the form of snow, but to convert that snow into usable water requires effort, stove time and fuel.

Generally in winter you need to cook and eat faster and give much more forethought to *what* you eat. The surface on which you cook is unstable and wet, calling for some different techniques to keep stoves working well and pots from tipping over.

Energy output is far greater for those who travel in snow, because of the need to keep body furnaces going without much external help from the sun and the fact that the work is often harder. Days are shorter and nights longer and colder, and that affects what is eaten and when.

There are plenty of positive factors that make some parts of the job easier and more fun. Designing and carving out a comfortable kitchen is exclusively a snow camper's treat, and results in a much homier, fancier setting than many summer camps afford. (My students have sculpted some works of art, complete with counters, benches, evergreen centerpiece, "wine cellar" for the fuel bottles, and a keystone arch highlighting the magnificent view!)

Appetites are hearty and diners appreciative. Many foods that aren't practical to carry on mild-weather trips make dandy winter fare, since you're traveling in a huge refrigerator. Even if you get careless and happen to spill your dinner when an unstable pot tips over, quick action can often rescue much of it from the clean snow that forms the kitchen counter. When the meal is over, cleanup is easier in handy, abrasive snow.

The winter wilderness is stunning in its beauty and impact on one who travels in it, but it is also much less forgiving than the same land in summer. Mistakes may mean not just discomfort, but a threat to survival. With a much narrower margin for error, the winter traveler needs to take even more care in his preparations for eating on the trail. But after all, you are there to have a satisfying experience, so any extra effort needed to gain that result should be accepted.

PLANNING YOUR BODY FUELS

Intake needs for food and water are somewhat different than in dirt camping, and meeting these needs is even more critical. A dehydrated or poorly fueled snow traveler becomes less energetic, more prone to hypothermia and frostbite, less able to function wisely and efficiently and less resilient should he become injured or ill.

DRINK. At least *3 to 4 quarts of liquid per day* are needed to replace that lost by excretion through the kidneys, perspiration and evaporation from the lungs. A snow trekker is apt to drink less than his summer counterpart because not only is water less available, but he also probably won't feel as consciously thirsty as when he is hot. (Thirst isn't an adequate guide as to what you need.) He'll need to force himself to tank up when he can, drinking a lot as well as filling water bottles. Soupy meals can provide liquid and salt to replace what's lost.

Some people are reluctant to drink as much as they should, thinking of the hassle of leaving a cozy bed during the night. One easy solution: Concentrate most liquid intake in the first half of the day. I drink till I slosh at breakfast—*at least* 5 or 6 cups of something hot—to get a good start on the day's quota.

Make getting water as easy as possible by camping near it whenever you can. On one very cold trip, I foolishly got dehydrated simply because of poor campsite choice . . . a scenic knoll a quarter mile from the nearest open stream. The days were so cold and windy that I didn't spend enough time melting snow; hence, my liquid needs went only half met. I paid in loss of stamina.

If you have to melt snow for water before fixing meals, you'll need to carry considerably more fuel (which, like water, weighs about 2 pounds per quart) and allow much more time for meal preparations.

Is eating snow safe? Yes, in moderate amounts, IF you're active, not chilled, warmly dressed, you melt it in your mouth before swallowing, and it's not yellow or pink. "Watermelon snow" gets it name from the pleasant taste and scent caused by microorganisms that can bring on diarrhea (a dehydrating condition best avoided anytime, but especially when snow trekking). Eating large amounts of snow at one time can dangerously lower the body's core temperature because of the energy required to convert the snow to liquid.

A word of caution about consuming alcoholic beverages on winter trips. In anything above the most conservative, careful dose, alcohol isn't wise for at least two reasons: (a) It dilates the surface blood vessels, creating the illusion of warmth while you're actually losing precious body heat; and (b) it dulls reflexes and judgment, both essential equipment for a successful snow trekker.

FOOD. Caloric needs are roughly 1,000 calories a day *more* than what a summer backpacker requires. Depending on size, weight, activity level and weather conditions, approximately 4,000 to 5,000 calories a day are needed when winter camping. The increased need results from the more strenuous level of activity and the fact that sources of warmth are usually only food, exercise and insulative clothing, with little help from the sun. (One of the many bonuses of winter camping is being able to eat all you want and not worry about gaining weight!)

About half the calories taken in should be in the form of carbohydrates and the remainder divided between fats and proteins, with more emphasis on fats. (See pages 5–6 for a discussion of these major food elements and their sources.)

Because of the body's need for more fats in cold weather, a skier or snowshoer who dislikes greasy foods such as sausage in summer may find them appealing in snow. Fats are a very efficient food, giving over twice as many calories per pound as either proteins or carbohydrates.

Paying attention to these increased needs, cold-weather campers use tuna packed in oil rather than water, don't drain the starch-laden cooking water from pasta (just add the sauce powder to it), swig Sherpa Tea, have an energy-producing snack at bedtime and some food handy during the night in case they wake up cold.

MENU PLANNING

Menu planning for snow revolves around two main considerations: food should be easy to prepare and have high caloric content for its weight. There's no room in your pack or your meal plans for "empty" foods that do little to fuel you.

Plan well in advance and thoroughly think through the preparation required for a food item as well as the results it will yield. Then you'll eat well on your journey while doing as little work in camp as necessary in as brief a time as possible.

Prepackage food at home where your warm fingers will do what you ask. In common with mild-weather trips, the food planner needs to consider: number of people, length of trip, variety needed, likes and dislikes, how much money to spend, how much preparation time is available. *The most critical factors to consider when planning snow food are:* the strenuous level of activity, probable weather conditions, availability of water and the usual need to cook and eat fast, with minimum hand motions. Some of the possible implications of these factors are:

- One-pot dishes mean fewer packages to open; they also stay hot while you eat.
- Foods that mix in resealable bags simplify cleanup.
- Since you'll do most of the preparation at home, fortify food whenever possible with extra dry milk, wheat germ, sunflower seed kernels, sesame seeds and such.
- Carry ample margarine and cheese in your general cooking supplies and add some to almost everything you cook, to give you the needed fats and proteins.
- When packaging, combine ingredients that can cook together whenever possible (example: put cereal to be cooked into a bag with dry milk, brown sugar and chopped fruit).
- Package all parts of a meal together, with simple directions written on freezer-tape labels in indelible ink. Everyone in the group should be able to prepare the food and run the stove!
- Use the quickest-cooking form of ingredients when you have a choice (such as *skinny* noodles, *10-minute* brown rice, *granular* TVP instead of chunks).
- On short trips where weight isn't a major factor, consider using foods such as canned meat with gravy as components of one-pot meals.
- Some use of freeze-dried foods can be worth the expense, since they shorten preparation time and require little fuss.

- Plan at least *some* "blizzard meals," which require no cooking and can be eaten in the warmth of your sleeping bag.

Food weights can be about the same as you would plan for a hiking trip, but usually are a little more. The weight of your other gear is probably more than in mild weather (heavier shelter, more clothing), but most people can comfortably carry more weight on skis than when hiking, once they get the knack of balancing well. Snowshoeing is more akin to hiking, however, and pack weight should be about what you can comfortably carry in mild weather. Be concerned not only with how much food weighs, but also with how *bulky* it is, since your pack will be fuller. Rely more on concentrated foods that give more calories for their weight and bulk.

EQUIPMENT PLANNING

Equipment for winter camp cooking should be easy to manipulate with gloves or mittens on and kept in good working order. Carry repair/replacement items and know how to use them.

Always take a stove, even if all your foods are no-cook. You'll at least need to boil water. For a group of three or more, carry two stoves so that one can heat water and the other do the cooking. A second stove is also a sensible safety precaution; it can take over for a malfunctioning first one. My winter stove preference is the old reliable Svea 123 with the addition of the Optimus Mini-Pump, which boosts power and makes it easier to start. This pump comes with a special fuel tank cap that replaces the stove's original one and is usable on the Optimus 8R or 99 as well as the Svea.

In a group it's always good to have a second stove such as the higher-powered Coleman Peak 1 or the MSR (Mountain Safety Research). Both stoves burn white gas or Coleman fuel. (Butane isn't a suitable winter fuel, since it won't vaporize below freezing.) A high-powered stove is great for melting snow, heating quantities of water and cooking foods that don't require very gentle heat.

Whatever your choice of stove, make sure it is stable and that pots set on it fit snugly and won't tip. A too-large pot on a tiny stove has caused dismay in many snow kitchens. The Optimus stove arrangement of tank and burner side by side gives stability, and so does the windscreen/cook kit set designed for use with the Svea (which by itself does not have a broad enough base to be stable on snow).

Estimate fuel needs generously, and carry at least enough for 2 hours' use per stove per day. Much stove time is spent heating water, an absolute necessity.

A valuable piece of equipment is a small square of closed-cell foam for under your stove (cut it just the right size) and another to stand or sit on while cooking. The larger one can double as insulation under the foot of your sleeping bag, where a three-quarter pad doesn't reach. The compact material insulates very well, so that snow doesn't draw heat from your stove or feet. (Outdoor stores sell stove-sized scraps of closed-cell foam, or you can cut your own from an old pad.)

For cooking, two nesting pans with lids (or foil substitutes) are usually adequate for up to three people. Take simple eating tools, such as two cups and a big spoon for each camper. If your spoons are the white Lexan ones (popular because they're sturdy), use an indelible marker to add some color to the handles. This can save you a trip back to the spot after the spring thaw. Someone should make colored spoons for snow campers! In winter, compact plastic cups have definite advantages over larger, metal cups. They keep food hot longer and are easier to hold onto, hence less prone to spills. Some people like to eat from insulated cereal bowls and coffee mugs.

Water bottles should have *wide* mouths, which are easier to fill and not as quick to get plugged with ice. Tie a bootlace snugly around the neck and then knot the ends into a hanging loop several inches across. Slip your hand or a couple of fingers through the loop to keep from losing the bottle to an icy flow. Or, at a streambank that's a bit too high or corniced to allow safe approach, slip the loop over the handle of a ski pole and down to the basket. Now your arm is 4 feet longer!

An aid for getting and keeping water in camp is a lightweight collapsible bucket made of plastic-coated cloth (capacity 2½ gallons). When the only water is in a stream several feet below a corniced bank, this bucket can be tied to several feet of line, which is then affixed to the basket end of a ski pole; you are now set to go fishing for water you couldn't reach otherwise.

(The flexible watersack you use in summer isn't practical in very cold temperatures, nor can it be fished with.)

A large dark plastic garbage bag has many uses, one of which is as a solar still for collecting water. On warm afternoons when you make camp early, spread the bag in an open sunny spot and mold a large depression in the center. A closed-cell foam pad between snow and bag is helpful but not necessary. Spread a thin layer of *clean* snow on the rest of the bag, go off to play, and when you return, the melted snow will have formed several quarts of water for you, without the use of stove and fuel. I've safely used this "snow water" without any subsequent boiling, but I'm always careful to dig down several inches for the cleanest snow.

Bottom-filling plastic tubes work well for honey, jam and peanut butter except in very cold weather, when the contents become too solid to squeeze out. (I sometimes float a tube in the tea water or warm it near my body.)

My cleanup tools are simple: a few paper towels (for wiping out dishes), a small tube of biodegradable camp suds, and a piece of scouring pad. Most often none of these is used, because abrasive snow is a most efficient scrubber.

An inexpensive but most helpful item to tuck into your winter cooking supply bag is a pair of lightweight latex gloves (available at drug, variety and household supply sections). Buy them large enough to wear over wool gloves during tasks that require dexterity but can also get your gloves wet. They are great for cooking, getting water, cleaning dishes (and, incidentally, for sculpting snow kitchens, building trenches and putting up and taking down tents).

Other items for the general kitchen bag are: an army-type can opener, matches wrapped to stay dry, salt and pepper, coffee, tea and sometimes some cooking oil. All my food and cooking gear (except stove and fuel flask) ride in a treasured piece of equipment: a packcloth duffel bag with a zipper down the side and two small pockets inside. Everything is together, handy and easily protected from the elements . . . real virtues in snow camp.

COOKING TECHNIQUES

These involve attention to the problems of cold, moisture, instability of the cooking surface and the need for speed and efficiency.

- Choice of campsite affects the ease and safety of cooking. Stop early, while there is still some sun and people are not exhausted (that can mean 3:30 on a December trip!). Seek a spot sheltered from winds, not in a potential avalanche area or under dead trees or trees laden with snow ready to plop down. Camp near water whenever practical.
- If it isn't snowing, raining, or windy ... with skis, snowshoes or boots, pack down an area for the kitchen, leaving a raised "counter" which is also packed. Pack a path between tents and kitchen.
- You might cook behind the shelter of a small windscreen—a tarp or space blanket strung vertically between trees, strategically placed packs, or a windwall built of snow. A trench kitchen is very protected.
- More elaborate, but a good investment of time and energy (especially for a base camp) is a genuine *sculpted snow kitchen.* It provides comfort and convenience for both cooks and diners and can be roofed for protection from snow or rain. Under a tarp, warm bodies and the heat from stoves can make this wilderness room downright cozy!

  With shovels, dig down several feet to form a broad table surrounded by benches. A large tarp can be hung over the whole kitchen, peaked in the middle for runoff. (Stand a ski upright in the center of the table.)
- Some folks cook inside their tents or light their stoves outside and then bring them in. I prefer to keep all cooking outside, at least 2 or 3 feet from the nearest tent. My main reason is safety. One tipped-over stove or faulty safety valve would destroy my wilderness home. There is also carbon monoxide poisoning to consider. Aside from these serious factors, I'm just too untidy a cook for indoors! Soup or pudding on clothes, sleeping bag or other gear can take the edge off snow pleasure.

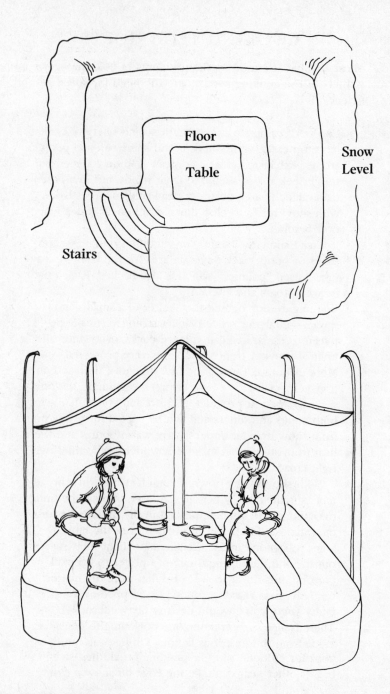

Floor

Table

Snow
Level

Stairs

And cooking in even a well-ventilated tent increases the amount of condensation collecting on inside walls.

- Have all cooking needs handy before starting to cook. The fewer motions around stoves, the less danger of knocking them over. Even the simple act of asking someone to bring an item from a pack is different here, when ears are covered with ski hats and sound-absorbing snow is all around.
- Set your stove on a piece of closed-cell foam, making sure it is stable. If using two stoves, keep them fairly close together so that each benefits from the other's warmth. While cooking, stand or sit on another piece of foam.
- Try to keep from spilling food, especially on mittens or other gear that won't be easy to clean or dry out.

  Above all, don't spill fuel . . . instant frostbite on your skin!
- Wipe moisture from the sides and bottoms of pans before setting them on a stove; otherwise it beads at the center and falls on the burner. One drop can put out a Svea!
- Always carry starter water for melting snow. Have about an inch of water in the pan, adding snow slowly. Otherwise, snow will blot up water as it forms, resulting in a scorched taste. If you have no starter water, hold the pan a bit above the flame until enough snow has melted to collect at least a half inch in the bottom

  Use the most compact snow or ice available. It takes *buckets* of fluffy powder to produce a quart of water. Dense compacted snow, crusty snow and icicles all melt into a greater volume of liquid.
- Think ahead to morning water needs when cooking the evening meal, and melt what water you'll want for starting breakfast.
- When fixing meals at much below freezing, you even need to give thought to keeping water thawed as you cook. Set waiting bottles and pans of water on insulating pads.
- As you fill water bottles from a pan, first set the bottle

in a lid or empty pan. Any precious water that misses the bottle is then salvageable.

- On a warm day set pans to catch drips of water from rocks and overhanging snowbanks or melt water with a solar still.
- If weather dictates cooking from the doorway of a tent so that you can stay warm and dry, first collect a supply of clean snow in a trash bag to keep handy for melting into water.
- A word about water purity. The protozoan bad guy *Giardia lamblia* is known to survive in cyst form in very cold water for months. So it can be present in the purest-looking backcountry waters even in winter. To avoid the resulting intestinal disease, boil water vigorously for 1 minute.
- Clean up by using snow to scrub food from pans. Don't wait until the food is frozen, though. Dispose of leftovers right after meals. The summer tactic of saving half the applesauce for breakfast won't work unless temperatures are mild.
- After your stove has cooled down following evening chores, top up the fuel tank for its next use . . . one less task for morning, when your fingers will be cold.
- Carry margarine or butter in chunk form in plastic bags or other containers rather than the plastic tubes, which are fine for mild weather. Frozen margarine won't squeeze out worth a darn!
- At take care to keep food and liquids from freezing: Bury them deep in your pack, or at least pile stuffsacks full of other gear around food items. Some folks take water bottles to bed with them.
- On very cold nights, wrap the bottle in a sock and take the additional precaution of storing it *upside down.* Then, if ice forms, it won't be plugging the neck.
- If toes and fingers are cold when you turn in for the night, holding them next to a bottle of water is the quickest thawout!
- Be sure you have some liquid available in each tent at night. A headache is hard to cure without something to wash an aspirin down.

- Have food handy for nighttime snacks...ten or twelve hours is a long time to be inactive in the cold, and isometrics can generate only so much heat.
- A tent large enough to accommodate your pack makes great sense. Nothing need be left outside to disappear under a fresh snowfall, be eaten by critters or freeze up. It's a real drag to leave your snug bed and tent to retrieve some item you need from your pack.

SNOW FOOD IDEAS

What foods work well in snow? The ideal is something easy to fix, easy to eat and not messy. First, go through your summer repertoire and make a list of foods that are simplest to fix, heartiest in terms of both energy produced and a lift to the spirits. Remember to stress high caloric content for the weight of the food item. Your list might include:

Breakfast

Familia
granola
instant cereals
English muffins
granola bars
breakfast bars
prebaked muffins
bacon bar
meat sticks
raisins
dried fruit
fruit leather

dehydrated honey
powdered juice
instant coffee
tea
instant cocoa
instant breakfast drink
Ovaltine
hot fruit drinks (lemonade, etc.)
hot fruit gelatin
powdered eggnog drink
powdered spiced cider

Lunch and Snacks

jerky

salami

smoked or dried fish

sturdy bread

sturdy crackers

peanut butter

condensed mincemeat

pemmican bars

cheese

bagels

rolls

energy bars

Mealpack bars

nuts

trail mix

candy

Dinner

powdered soup (instant best)

bouillon

quick rice

couscous

ramen noodles

instant potatoes

quick noodle dinners

frozen vegetables

freeze-dried vegetables

canned meats

freeze-dried meats

meat bar

sour-cream sauce mix

freeze-dried entrees

precooked (at home) meats

instant pudding

fruitcake

fig and apricot bars

prebaked brownies

prebaked individual dessert cakes

Home-dried foods (see chapter 19) are especially useful, and learning to prepare them can add a creative dimension to your adventuring.

Freeze-dried foods sometimes have a place in snow camp menus because they are lightweight, quick and relatively easy to prepare, but a steady diet of them for more than a weekend gets dull and may cause digestive upsets. It is also very expensive.

Explore the grocery store, natural foods store, outdoor store, ethnic market and import store with an eye to what foods could be adapted to snow camp use.

When weight is not a crucial factor (such as on a weekend trip), some canned foods that contain liquid can be welcome additions to your menu: individual puddings, meats, poultry and fish that is packed with sauce or gravy.

Some foods work *better* in cold weather, such as perishable meats and vegetables that might spoil in summer. Using chunks of leftover roast in a one-pot main dish is practical in winter, whereas it could be dangerous on very hot summer trips. Hamburger, precooked at home to reduce bulk, mess and preparation time, fortifies soup and many main dishes.

Just be sure the perishables you carry can be kept from freezing! The best place to assure this is deep in your pack (the same place that keeps things cool in summer).

Hot fruit gelatin to drink is a very satisfying dessert and boosts a camper's liquid intake. Heated with fruit soup mix from the import store, it is doubly fortifying. A rich, rich "drink" is instant pudding you've heated up.

Develop a good range of one-pot main dishes that can be varied by changing one or two ingredients. Chapter 10, "The One-Liner," will provide ideas for hundreds of combinations. Just remember to use the quickest-cooking forms of ingredients in combinations that require few hand motions and preparation steps. When creating a one-liner, remember that the quickest-cooking carbohydrate bases are instant mashed potaotoes, couscous and ramen noodles, and the quickest sauces are instant soups.

Many people who prefer to avoid the expense of freeze-dried foods in milder weather will include them in at least some snow meal plans, perhaps with the added zip of a favorite spice blend. If you don't want to use main dishes, use a freeze-dried meat or vegetable ingredient in combination with grocery store ingredients. This tactic can speed preparation time and average out total costs to a more reasonable level.

Many high-energy, no-cook snack foods can be prepared ahead at home and used as pick-me-ups while traveling, as part of a no-cook breakfast, as desserts with lunch or dinner and as bedtime snacks.

The range of food possibilities for snow camping is infinite! Once you begin exploring what's available, and how to combine, package and prepare foods for use in the winter wilderness, you'll find ideas coming so thick and fast that you'll be snow camping more than ever.

These recipes, found elsewhere in the book, are especially well suited to snow camp use:

BEVERAGES

Rich Trail Cocoa (107)
Sherpa Tea (108)
Mexican Mocha (108)
Russian Tea (107)
Spiced Hot Milk (109)
Hot Malt (109)
Carob–Malt Smoothie (110)
Instant Breakfast Drinks (129)
Spiced Coffee (130)

BREAKFAST

Sunrise Spuds (59)
Probars (59)
Grandola Bars (60)
Protein-Power Cereal (61)
Sesame–Raisin Wakeup (61)
Spotted Applesauce (62)
Breads: Pumpkin, Zucchini, Cranberry, Sweet Wheat
and Raisin, Spicy Apple (63–65)
Instant Oatmeal (128)

LUNCH AND SNACKS

Indestructible Cornmeal Rounds (68)
Zippy Herbed Crackers (68)
Ham-and-Cheese-Filled Biscuits (69)
Quick Curried Soup (70)
Gorp (100)
Mountain Bars (101)
Gorp Squares (101)
Fruit Balls (102)
Peanut Butter Supercookies (102)
Honey–Nut Bars (103)
Butterscotch Brownies (104)
Logan Bread (104)
Pemmican (105)
Peanut Butter Spread (132)
Sesame Honeys (133)
Singular Sausage (134–135)
Jerkies (meat, fish, poultry) (148–150)

DINNER

many One-Liners (pages 82–92); choose ones
where all or most ingredients cook together; check
the "Quick" and "Light" lists on pages 91–92
Cheesy Bacospuds (75)
Sunset on the Plains (76)
Bouillabaisse (77)
Rice and Vegetable Dinner Mix (78)

DESSERT

No-cook desserts (93–94)
Fruit Stacks (94)
Cheesecake (95)
Traveling Grasshopper Pie (95)
Quick Rice Desserts (96)
Stewed Fruit Compote (96–97)
Apple–Peach Crunch (97)
Molasses Marbles (132)

Index

June Fleming, who lives in Portland, Oregon, has taught classes in backpacking and snow camping for ten years and has led hundreds of trips in the Cascade Mountain range and other parts of the Pacific Northwest. Her Backcountry Kitchen segments were seen as part of the 1984 public television series, "The Great Outdoors" produced by WGBH Boston.